The Meeting Place
Aboriginal Life In Toronto

in celebration of the

Native Canadian Centre of Toronto's

35th Anniversary

Edited by
Frances Sanderson &
Heather Howard-Bobiwash

Published by the Native Canadian Centre of Toronto

Copyright © 1997 by Native Canadian Centre of Toronto

Canadian Cataloguing in Publication Data

Main entry under title:

    The meeting place: aboriginal life in Toronto

In celebration of the Native Canadian Centre of
    Toronto's 35th anniversary.
Includes bibliographic references and index.
ISBN 0-9682546-0-8

    1. Indians of North America--Ontario--Toronto.
2. Indians of North America--Ontario--Toronto--Social
conditions. I. Sanderson, Frances, 1949- II. Howard-
Bobiwash, Heather, 1966- III. Native Canadian Centre
of Toronto.

E78.O5M43 1997   305.897'0713541   C97-900788-7

Published by
Native Canadian Centre of Toronto
16 Spadina Rd.
Toronto, Ontario, Canada, M5R 2S7

To order, call:
(416) 964-9087

Printed and bound in Canada by:
Printart Design Consultants Inc., Toronto, Ontario

Table of Contents

Cover Image

"Hope" by Maxine Noel

We very gratefully acknowledge Maxine Noel for her generous donation to the Native Canadian Centre of Toronto of the painting entitled, "Hope" which appears on the cover of this book. Maxine Noel is a Dakota artist. Some early exhibition of her work took place at the Native Canadian Centre of Toronto, and she is now a well-known artist nationally and internationally. Here is her own interpretation of this piece:

A very dear friend, Cecil Youngfox, once gave me a tour of the Native Canadian Centre of Toronto. He wanted to introduce me to the people who ran this wonderful Centre and show me the artwork that hangs there. He felt that the Centre had great potential; that it was a place where our people could meet in learning, in sharing, in times of trouble, and in times of celebration. He felt that as artists, we should give back some of our gifts in any way we could. In that respect, in this painting, I would like to immortalize my friend Cecil Youngfox and his dream of hope for our people through the transitions we make as we travel towards the millennium, keeping our traditional ways, and thereby being better prepared for what lies ahead.

Maxine Noel

Introducing the "Meeting Place"

Frances Sanderson

This book presents a landscape of urban Aboriginal history and culture. It provides a close examination from a variety of perspectives: scholars and members of the Native community in Toronto, family histories and personal experiences. Sections of this book deal with the chronological record of events, while others relate personal glimpses of individual lives demonstrating the resourcefulness and true spirit of the Anishnawbe people.

Many years ago explorers came to this great country looking for something they were not to find. There were no gold or jewels littering the countryside. This land was certainly not the short route to the "Orient." Nothing could validate their expeditions except conquering people with cultures that were open, friendly and focused on living a good, communal way of life. This "new found" civilization of people was intent on survival. Although survival was not their mainstay, it was a result of their lifestyle.

Anishnawbe people have a deep-rooted respect for Mother Earth and all that she provides. This respect has been significant in the unselfish way that Aboriginal people have shared their knowledge of the land and treated newcomers to their territories. Native people believe in taking only what they need, treating others with respect and honouring their families. This respect is filtered to everyone through their writings, art, and prayers.

Prayers are said at all special occasions and more importantly on a personal daily basis. Prayers thank the Creator for supplying all that is necessary to sustain life on Mother Earth. No creature is too big or too small for inclusion in our appreciation. Every aspect of Nature is acknowledged, the plants, the animals, the fishes, the birds, the water, the fire, the wind, the rain, the snow, the sun, the daylight, the moon, the darkness of night, and

Mother Earth.

Prayers, although they are nondenominational, reflect the respect and reverence Native people have for the Great Creator and all that he has provided. This respect for an all-powerful and benevolent being came to be quickly criticized by those touting Christianity in the "New" world. The beliefs of Native people were invalidated, and it was assumed that the Creator represented idol worship. In actual fact, Aboriginal people were far more pious than those who came in boat loads to change the complexion of the land and "convert the Natives."

Native people welcomed all to their fireside. Initially Anishnawbe were perhaps the innocent, unsuspecting hosts to those who would try and change their lives. Aboriginal philosophy stressed tolerance, respect and open friendliness. Until those virtues were destroyed, everyone was afforded the opportunity to live in harmony with their Native hosts.

Much has been written about the early settlers and what they brought to this land, and little attention is paid to the fact that the early Aboriginal people here had already settled and "tamed" the great land. They were on the beaches to greet the newcomers as they floundered ashore. Anishnawbe people were critical to the well-being of these new settlers. They taught them how to live off the land. The Anishnawbe were quick to share their knowledge of hunting, fishing, and agriculture. The foreigners were instructed in weather conditions, how to prepare and keep food for the long, cold winters. The Anishinawbe were the benefactors of these weary, unprepared colonists. The Toronto area has long been a meeting place for Aboriginal people, as historians have documented over the years. It is fitting that today's Native people have reclaimed their land in this area, in small parts, by setting up groups, associations, agencies and organizations dotting the landscape of Toronto, and making their presence known.

The pages in this book not only describe the historic circumstances surrounding the existence of Aboriginal people, but tell the tales of the people who now call the *Meeting Place*, Toronto, home. It is of prime value that these histories recount the relevancy of traditional values and culture and how they played a role in the migrations of Native people to this area. We find that the Aboriginal community is tightknit, and still unconquered after all the years of supposed (forced) assimilation.

The Anishnawbe People have clung to each other for support throughout their existence. Many have one foot firmly planted on reserve land, the other in the city. These bi-cultural Aboriginal philosophers have guided Native people through the maze of civility, European thinking and urban development. They have acted as shepherds, gently nudging their flocks toward cultural freedom in the urban setting while keeping them focused on the traditional values and teachings that have been the grounding on which Aboriginal identity is based.

The Native Canadian Centre of Toronto was of prime importance in the early, formative years of the urban Native community, and continues to be a focal point. It is place to meet, have socials and discuss the future. Many organizations and agencies got their footing and support from their association with the Centre. It was a place that nurtured, educated, disciplined and supported the early Native residents of Toronto the city. It was a beacon on the horizon for many, offering a warm, homelike atmosphere that was essential for all.

Anishnawbe people came to the city for various and sundry reasons. When Native people, forced to reside on government-designated reservations, found that the regulations on their lives offered poor prospects for farming, fishing, hunting and survival, they migrated to the cities. When world wars broke out in 1914 and again in 1939, many Anishnawbe people joined up to fight for democracy, their homeland, their families, as well as to honour treaties with peoples they had considered to be their allies. Unfortunately, when Native people enlisted, they also lost their rights as Aboriginal people, including the right to residency in their homes on reserves. Often, the only recourse for survival was to remain in the city.

Young Native people thirsting for knowledge were also forced to give up their recognition as Aboriginal people when they entered into universities. Some youngsters and wee babies were taken from their families and loved ones by the church in an effort to speed up the assimilation process and convert them into mainstream-thinking Canadians. There are many reasons why Native people congregated in

3

urban centres and most people, today, would say their subsequent treatment was unjust. When all these circumstances are combined, it is easy to see why the Native population in metropolitan locations exploded. What might not be so obvious is the strength, vitality, and solidarity that these conditions also created.

The stories of urban Aboriginal life in this book concentrate on the vibrancy and resilience of the community. They tell of how Anishnawbe people clung together for support, how they solidified with a feeling of purpose. Personal stories recount and highlight the symbiotic relationships that span the myriad of Native and non-Native cultures that pervade the city. They also tell of the long and tenuous journeys that many have made to get to this point in time.

Who are the urban Aboriginal people of Toronto? They are our history, our memory, our Elders, grandfathers, grandmothers, aunties, uncles, mothers, fathers, brothers, sisters and children. They are visible in the family circles, gatherings, socials and pow wows. They are the foundations for all the organizations, associations and agencies that have sprung up, in and around Toronto, the Meeting Place. They are where you least expect to find them, and they are in the most likely places; they are your friends, neighbours, teachers, doctors, dentists, and police personnel. They have a staying power unlike any other, but are as fragile as the most delicate crystal. They are strong and powerful, and sensitive and kind. They are friendly and welcoming, but dignified and austere. They are wise and complicated while being logical and realistic. They are my people.

The History of Native People in the Toronto Area, An Overview

A. Rodney Bobiwash

Prior to Settlement

For Aboriginal people living in the Toronto area there is a long history of Native occupation which Toronto's modern towers of concrete and steel may obscure but cannot eradicate. The Toronto Islands were important stopping places for the Native fishery and were described as places of healing and spiritual renewal. During the fur trade Aboriginal people camped there while trading furs at Fort Rouille (one of a series of three French fur trade posts at Toronto) and later Fort York. Prior to the arrival of white traders and missionaries in the area Champlain had described it as a land of "pleasing character."[1] The Toronto area offered a rich habitat both for Aboriginal societies practising hunting and gathering (and later fur trading and trapping) and those pursuing agricultural/horticultural activities.

There is much evidence that when European explorers first penetrated the interior of North America they found broad park-like forest areas. This led to the mistaken belief that North American forests were proto-forests, or primordial forests. In fact, the park-like forest expanses were carefully managed and cultivated horticultural storehouses for Native people.[2] The Toronto area supported many different types of habitat which in turn supported various forms of wildlife such as fish, beaver, muskrats and frogs in the rivers, streams and lakes, deer and caribou in the forest, and various kinds of fowl in the trees. The waterways also provided natural travel routes, and there were many fine harbours and lees to find shelter in. It has been posited by some historical researchers that pre-contact

5

Aboriginal people in North America were the original "affluent society." By this they meant that, compared to other societies at that time, the amount of time Aboriginal people had to spend to fulfill their subsistence needs was less therefore leaving more time for leisure and other cultural, recreational and social pursuits. In the Toronto area there is no doubt that the climate, moderated by the Great Lakes, and the abundance of foodstuffs available bears out this thesis. According to William Dean,

> The Great Lakes moderate to some degree Ontario's climate of extremes. They retard the warming of the surrounding land in spring and early summer because the water remains cool. They also extend the autumn season by retaining their summer warmth. In all seasons, the Lakes are an important source of precipitation throughout the year... because of these favourable climactic conditions, the Native people of the southern parts could engage in horticulture.[3]

Or as noted somewhat more poetically by Enimekeese in 1867,

> Not many generations have passed away since the "red man" was lord of all America. At that time his throne was the highest peak of the mountains. His fields, gardens, and pleasure grounds were the extended plains and immense forests, with hill and dale, vale and valley, interspersed with beautiful lakes, and diversified with endless sweeping, rolling, rushing rivers.
>
> There was but little to torture or vex the mind, nothing seemed to disquiet them, or disturb their repose. In their several tribes they generally lived at peace with each other. They roamed the vast forest in perfect freedom, and enjoyed life and liberty without interruption.

They were active in the chase, and fortunately they had an abundance of game to pursue. Verily, they were surrounded with the luxuries and comforts of life, and had all the game and fruits of the soil they required...4

It is estimated that Aboriginal people living in the north central Great Lakes region utilized as many as 400 different plant species for items as diverse as snowshoes, baskets, clothing, shelter, transportation, warmth, food, medicine, and ceremonial purposes.5

Archaeologists have labeled the original inhabitants of the Toronto area as the "Clovis" people. They are believed to have been large game hunters, and inhabited the area between 9,000 B.C. and 5,000 B.C., a time period referred to by archaeologists as the "Paleo-Indian Period." According to archaeologists then, people have continuously occupied the Toronto area for about 11,000 years. The Great Lakes area, particularly around Toronto, was a place not dissimilar to the Mediterranean in the Old World in that many cultures and peoples met for the purposes of trade and commerce, dating back thousands of years prior to European contact. In this process, cultures melded and developed, groups intermarried and languages and cultures flourished. Opportunities to simultaneously pursue agriculture and game hunting meant that the Native peoples of the area had the luxury of developing complex and sophisticated ceremonial lives; the long autumn season was and is an important ceremonial time in the annual cycles of all of the Aboriginal peoples who have lived in the region. The Mississauga (who refer to themselves as Anishnawbe, and are also known as Ojibway or Chippewa) tell of how they came from the east and were led by a sacred Megis shell into "the good land," the western Great Lakes area. Eddie Benton Benai summarizes the story of this migration in *The Mishomis Book*,

> In the time of the first fire, the Anishinabe nation will rise up and follow the Sacred Shell... the sacred Megis will lead the way to the chosen ground of the Anishinabe. You are to look for a turtle-shaped island that is linked to the

purification of the Earth. You will find such an island at the
beginning and end of your journey. There will be seven
stopping places along the way. You will know that the
chosen ground has been reached when you come to a
land where food grows on water...[6]

While the final resting place of the Anishnawbe was farther to the west
there is no doubt that the Toronto Islands were a stopping place along the
migration route and later the Mississaugas were to reclaim this land as
territory of their own. Among the teachings around the Great Migration is
the teaching that in those places the Anishnawbe stopped they established
villages and left people behind as they traveled onwards.

Archaeologists have labeled another period of human occupation
in the area, from 1,000 B.C. to the time of European contact, as the
"Woodland Period." The Toronto area specifically falls within an area
referred to by the archaeologists as the Point Peninsula, a cultural area
defined in terms of the interpretations of the type of material or artifacts
found in the region. People in this cultural area developed extensive trading
networks with items found in archaeological digs from as far away as the
Ohio Valley, the Gulf of Mexico, the north shore of Lake Superior, James
Bay, and the Plains area. They developed elaborate burial mounds (i.e.
The Serpent Mounds) and sophisticated pottery and metal-working
techniques. Three major cultural groups have been identified to have
occupied the area encompassing eight distinct tribal groups: The Iroquois
(Huron, Petun, Neutral and Erie); the St. Lawrence Iroquois — a group
distinct from the former; and, the Algonquian (Cree, Ojibway and
Algonquin).[7] There were doubtless many other tribal peoples who traveled
and traded in the area but did not establish a permanent presence.

It is certain that extensive trading networks had been established
across the Americas well before the arrival of Europeans. In North America
the most elaborate network (supported by many smaller local trade
networks) was mediated largely by Mandan peoples in the Plains area.
This network stretched from Mexico to James Bay, and from the Atlantic
coast to the Pacific. Some archaeological digs carried out in the Toronto

area unearthed artifacts which originated on the Pacific coast. The typical path of an artifact of this sort might have been that it was traded by West Coast people to Native people in the interior of what is now British Columbia, such as the Salish. From there it may be traded across the Kootenay with the Blackfoot who in turn would trade with the Mandan. The Mandan traded the object with the people of the Mississippi, the Miami for example, who would then trade it to people in the upper Great Lakes, and the item would find its way to the people of the Toronto area. The importance of the trade network was not only in the procurement of goods from other areas but in the establishment of relationships with other peoples, in the exchange of information, and in the apprehension of knowledge about people and places far beyond their immediate environs. All of this would stand them in good stead when they encountered non-Native people.

Early Stages of Contact with Europeans

While there was little direct contact between the people of the Toronto area and early colonists on the Atlantic seaboard there was undoubtedly knowledge very early on of both the French to the north and east and the early Dutch and English colonists to the south-east. The Aboriginal peoples of the eastern seaboard in what is now New England entered into agreements with colonists to protect them and feed them and to have them live peaceably in their lands.[8] This relationship was symbolized in different ways. The most famous of these agreements was demonstrated in the Two Row Wampum of the Six Nations. Wampums were belts of shells or beads which recorded the history of agreements. They were used as mnemonic and teaching devices and a great many were made to commemorate treaties between different First Nations and between Native and non-Native peoples. For instance, the Hiawatha Belt depicts the founding of the Haudonesaunee Confederacy with two nations represented by rectangles on either side of the Onondaga, the Firekeepers, who are represented by a pine tree.[9] The Two Row Wampum depicted two boats sailing beside each other in a straight line. The lesson was clear that each nation would travel together as long as it was beneficial to each but that each would remain in their own vessel neither interfering with the other. This wampum truly embodied the relationship as it was expected to develop between settlers and Aboriginal people from an Aboriginal perspective.

The other major symbol used by both the Haudonesaunee and the Anishnawbe to define the relationship between themselves and the settlers was the Covenant Chain. The Covenant Chain was originally used to represent the relationship established between the Dutch and First Nations. Each party was to hold one end of the chain and it was not to be broken. However, it is said that this chain was made of iron and over time it rusted and deteriorated, and eventually was broken. The next chain, established between the British and First Nations, was made of silver so that when it would become tarnished it could be polished, and the relationship would shine as brightly as it had when first established. In the Covenant Chain both parties were required to hold fast to the chain and if either dropped their end the relationship would be broken. Like the two Row Wampum the Covenant Chain entrenched a relationship of mutual respect, consideration, and trust between Native and non-Native nations.

The Period of European Exploration and Settlement

The first non-Native visitors to the Toronto area were fur traders and missionaries in the early 1600s. Significant amounts of European trade goods, however, had reached the Great Lakes area well ahead of these explorers, at least half of a century before[10] and some trade goods had doubtless reached the area even earlier in trade from the Atlantic coast. The first non-Native person to reach the "big beautiful lake" was likely the French courier-de-bois Etienne Brule, whose first view was from the mouth of the Humber River in 1615.[11] Brule, recorded no human habitation at that time and it is thought that the villages in this area had been abandoned about half-a-century earlier. It is very likely, however, that the rich mouths of the rivers flowing into Lake Ontario were used at the very least on an annual basis by the Anishnawbe to harvest fish. Archaeologists also think that a large village known as Teiaiagon at Toronto was established, about fifty years after Brule's visit, by the Seneca on the Humber River about two-and-one-half kilometres north of Lake Ontario (now just south of High Park). This village was recorded by Father Hennepin in November 1678 who visited it after his ship was blown ashore during a storm.[12]

The Jesuit missionaries arrived in the region in a concentrated effort in the 1640s, a time which coincided with the sweep of local epidemics through the Aboriginal populations. At this time it was estimated that approximately 65,000 Iroquoian people lived in the area[13] and that about fifty percent (50%) of these died as a result of the introduction of European diseases.[14] The death of so many people had predictable results: Many of the dead were elders and the communities were robbed of their leadership at a time it was most needed; productive capacity was severely diminished; the local positions of these Aboriginal people within the fur trade and within Native trading networks were undermined; and the inability of their own spiritual practitioners to deal with the foreign disease led to the undermining of Native spirituality. In sum the Native society was left demoralized and weakened by the effects of an alien epidemiology. By the 1750s the Iroquoian people of the Great Lakes area were scattered among the Algonquian-speaking people, primarily the Ottawa people. The French established a fur trade post called Fort Rouille in 1750 at what is now the site of the Canadian National Exhibition. The period of French exploration and trade was significant in laying the foundation for constitutional recognition of the inherent right of self-government by Native people.

From the earliest stages of French settlement in Canada, evidence of the acknowledgment of the independent status of Aboriginal peoples and their capacity to conclude treaties of peace and friendship were demonstrated. Early French representatives of the King were under orders to scrupulously uphold and observe treaties, provided the Aboriginal peoples and their leaders did the same. It was hoped that through these treaties, the fledgling fur trade between the French and their Aboriginal allies would flourish to the exclusion of rival trading powers such as the Dutch and the English.[15] The French had little interest in settlement outside of the St. Lawrence Valley and much interest in commerce with Native people, along with an interest in converting souls to Christianity. This lack

11

Bobiwash

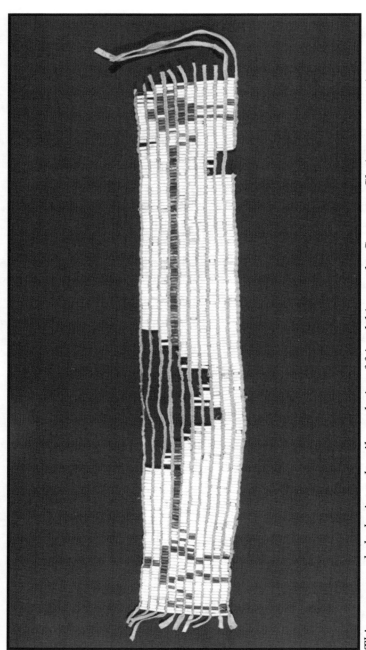

This wampum belt depicts the silver chain of friendship, as the Covenant Chain was sometimes called, linking the Native person on the right and the European on the left. Photograph by Richard Garner, The Covenant Chain: Indian Ceremonial Trade Silver; (Ottawa: National Museum of Man, 1980), p. 19. Reproduced with permission of the Canadian Museum of Civilization.

of interest in establishing settlements on Aboriginal lands and recognition of the advantages of mutually beneficial trading relationships led to the development of particular and harmonious relationships among Aboriginal peoples of the area and European peoples.

The French policy of cultivating friendship and alliance with Aboriginal peoples was emulated, with a lesser degree of success, in the British Colonies to the south. However, unlike the French, the British tendency was to compete for territory with their Aboriginal neighbours. War often resulted leading to the forcible dispossession of the Aboriginal nations from their lands. Over time, British settlement policy moved away from that of removal by force to that of securing lands by formal agreement with the Aboriginal occupants.[16] By 1763, British-Aboriginal relations had stabilized to the point where two fundamental principles had emerged:

a) Aboriginal peoples were generally recognized as autonomous political units capable of holding treaty relations with the Crown; and

b) Aboriginal nations were entitled to the territories in their possession unless or until they ceded them away.[17]

The British Crown's policies towards the Aboriginal peoples and the territories recently ceded by France and Spain were set out in the Royal Proclamation of 1763. The Imperial government had sought to bring management of all Indian Affairs in British North America under it's own purview and out of the hands of colonial authorities in 1755. The Royal Proclamation devoted fully one-third of it's text to matters relating to Aboriginal people. The Royal Proclamation defined the boundaries of new colonies in North America and marked the end of British-French hostilities in North America with the defeat of the French on the Plains of Abraham by General Wolfe. The Proclamation acknowledged the existence of self-contained Aboriginal nations holding their lands under the force of the British Proclamation and maintaining independent relations with the Crown. The Proclamation recognizes Aboriginal peoples as autonomous political units living under the Crown's protection, retaining both their internal political authority and their territories.[18]

From 1650-1710 southern Iroquois people had displaced other Iroquoian (Huron, Petun and Neutral) peoples from most of southern Ontario and the area had become a large hunting territory under the tenuous control of the Iroquois.[19] First Nations increasingly under pressure from European encroachment into their lands formed various alliances with European military and trading partners. What is important to remember is that Native people formed strategic alliances with both Europeans and other First Nations for their own purposes and with their own agendas. In 1762 the Ottawa Chief Pontiac formed a coalition of Ottawa, Potawatomi, Ojibway and Petun-Huron to force all Europeans out of the Western Great Lakes region. Although they captured a great many British forts they were not successful in capturing Detroit. Support from the French failed to materialize and in 1766 Pontiac was forced to conclude a treaty of peace and friendship with the British. Following Pontiac's war many Ottawa retreated to the Ohio valley and the south shore of Lake Michigan.

By the late eighteenth century land cessions, mostly negotiated under the terms of Peace and Friendship Treaties had laid the basis for increased European settlement of the Great Lakes region, and particularly the Toronto area. The region saw two great waves of immigration of foreign settlers, the first during and shortly after the American Revolutionary War (1776), and the second following the War of 1812. Around the year 1700, the Mississaugas had expelled the last of the Iroquois from the Toronto area and had re-established firm control and settlement of the north shore of Lake Ontario and the Trent River Valley. The first land surrender made by the Mississauga to the Crown was in 1781 where the Mississauga ceded land along the north bank of the Niagara River from Lake Erie to Lake Ontario in return for 300 suits of clothing. In 1783 the Mississauga negotiated the sale of the lands around the Bay of Quinte and lands along the shores of the Trent River and along the St. Lawrence River, near present-day Brockville. In 1783 the lands of the Grand River Valley were also sold to the British to be used by them as a reward for the Iroquois who had remained their allies during the American Revolution.

In 1785 John Collins, investigating a route across what was known as the "Toronto Carrying Place" (from the mouth of the Humber River to Lake Simcoe) apparently negotiated a provisional agreement to purchase a portion of the route. However, it appears that no formal agreement (as per the requirements of the Royal Proclamation of 1763) was ever made, that the description of the transaction is vague and unsubstantiated, and that the Mississaugas received no payment for the surrender.[20] In 1798 Governor Simcoe concluded an agreement with the Lake Simcoe Mississauga for a payment of 108 pounds which apparently included these lands. Another tract of land on the north shore of Lake Ontario between the Trent and Etobicoke Rivers, reaching back from Lake Ontario to Lake Simcoe, was also apparently expropriated illegally without regard for the processes established by the Royal Proclamation.

In 1787 and 1788 Sir John Johnson and Col. John Butler met with Aboriginal bands at the Carrying Place at both Quinte and Toronto. They apparently purchased a large tract of land on the north shore of Lake Ontario. However, the document which formalized the transaction omitted a description of the area surrendered. Instead, it contained a blank spot where descriptions of the surrendered land were supposed to be inserted after the fact. These irregularities were brought to the attention of Lord Dorchester (the Governor of Quebec) in 1794 by Lord Simcoe and Dorchester declared the document invalid. The matter remained dormant until 1916 when an Inquiry revealed that the lands remained unsurrendered, giving rise to the negotiation of and signing of the Williams Treaties in 1923.

In 1805 William Clark met with the Mississaugas at the Credit River and negotiated the sale of further lands including the site of the City of York. The Mississaugas agreed to surrender the land in exchange for 1,000£ (English Pounds) and the right to retain their fishery at the mouth of the Etobicoke River. They also sought to reserve the right to use of the Burlington Beach and fisheries at the mouth of the Credit River, Sixteen Mile Creek (Oakville), Twelve Mile Creek (Bronte), and other traditional fishing grounds. Interestingly enough, this agreement may have included Taddle Creek which ran through what is now "Philosopher's Walk" on

Bobiwash

TORONTO HARBOUR IN 1793.
(From an original drawing in the possession of Dr. Scadding, Toronto)

Toronto Harbour in 1793. Print (from original formerly in the collection of Dr. Scadding, Toronto) in the collection of the Canadian Decorative Arts Dept., Royal Ontario Museum. Reproduced with permission.

the St. George Campus of the University of Toronto.[21] It should be noted that the Mississaugas complained that settlers had harassed them and driven them off the shorelines of lands sold in the 1780s, in spite of the earlier assurances given by Col. John Butler that they would be protected against these incursions.[22] Clark noted that the Mississauga he met with appeared "thin and miserable" and their lands "lay dead."[23] It was obvious that years of disease, deprivation and harassment had taken their toll.

During this period, as settlement in the area accelerated, competition for game and other resources between settlers and Native peoples also increased resulting in escalating aggression against Native people. By 1796 the government had to pass *a Proclamation to Protect the Fishing Rights and the Burying Grounds of the Mississaugas*, forbidding settlers from harassing Native people harvesting fish at the mouths of rivers flowing into Lake Ontario (places that had been clearly reserved by the Mississaugas for this purpose), and to prevent settlers from looting Native burial grounds in search of artifacts and bones for sale. This *Proclamation* was largely ineffectual. As Peter Schmalz notes in his history of the Ojibway of Southern Ontario, nine years after it was passed Chief Kineubenac of the Credit River Mississaugas complained of a settler building a weir at the mouth of the river to catch salmon on their way upstream to spawn, and that the river was being polluted "by washing with soap and other dirt, that the fish refuse coming into the River as usual, by which our families are in great distress for want of food."[24]

The Reserve Period, 1835-1945

From the years 1815 to 1824 the non-Aboriginal population of Ontario doubled. At the same time the Mississauga population in some settlements had declined by more than fifty-percent as a result of disease. Pressure from settlement also resulted in a decline of game, making it increasingly difficult to live off the land. By this time Native people had ceased to be a significant political or military threat to settlement and found themselves increasingly deprived of their lands, participation in the polity of the new colony, and with little recourse. The inclusion of a Native person on the Coat of Arms of the City of Toronto in 1834 recognized the role of the Mississaugas in the history of the settlement.[25] However, that the person portrayed is obviously in Plains and not Mississauga dress, speaks clearly to the steady alienation of truth in the pursuit of a mythical history in which Aboriginal people, like the beaver adorning the top of the shield, were part and parcel of a subdued land and very much relegated to the past. The death of Techumseth in 1813 at the Battle of Moraviantown and the subsequent removal of Native people from their lands in the Detroit area by the American government signaled an ending of the powerful Aboriginal political confederacies which could negotiate with the American and Canadian governments. In 1855 a German visitor to Toronto Johann Georg Kohl noted that Native people,

> were numerous when the English founded here the town of York, and there are still people in Toronto who remember the fleets of bark canoes and little skiffs, in which the Indians used to bring fish and other things to sell to the inhabitants - mostly encamping on that long sandy peninsula... But the Indians have now vanished like the morning mist, and nothing remains to recall even their memory, but the well sounding name they invented for this locality - the sonorous Toronto.[26]

From 1830 to 1945 Native communities lived peaceably and developed some involvement in the life of Upper Canada. There were many protests launched by the them over illegal sales of Aboriginal lands and mistreatment by the officials of the Indian Department. In fact, corruption was so widespread in the Indian Department that in the 1830s and 1840s several independent commissions into corruption were held culminating in the *Bagot Commission* of 1841. Other protests centered upon the illegal alienation of Aboriginal lands; in 1860 the Mississaugas complained that their former Council Grounds, located where the Queen Street Mental Health Centre currently stands, still belonged to them. In a communication to the Duke of Newcastle in September 1860 they noted, "A lot of three acres in the vicinity of Toronto City near or where the Provincial Lunatic

Asylum now stands, this was a Reserve for camping and council purposes."[27]

Several Native converts to Methodism became prominent figures in the Christian movement and became missionaries both to their own people (the Ojibway) and to Aboriginal people further west and north (the Cree). These included Kahkewaquonaby "Sacred Feathers" or Peter Jones as he was known in English, Henry Bird Steinhauer who translated the New Testament into Ojibway, George Coppoway, John Sunday, Catherine Sunegoo Sutton, Peter Jacobs, George Henry and Alan Salt. By 1826 Chief Peter Jones and the Mississaugas of New Credit had built a "model village" at New Credit. The government, encouraged by the Methodist Mission Society, actively encouraged agricultural development in these "Christianized villages."

Native communities in which prominent Methodist leaders became Chiefs or assumed other leadership roles had become the so-called "Civilized tribes of the Chippewa" by the 1850s. Peter Jones at New Credit, John Sunday at Rama, Alan Salt at Parry Island, George Coppoway at Curve Lake — all worked to establish strong agricultural communities centered around school and church.

By the 1850s these communities had become so successful that their settler neighbours complained they had an unfair advantage in accessing the growing markets in York. Shortly thereafter the colonial government passed the first of a series of legislative acts designed to limit Native participation in the economic, social and political life of the colony, called the *Gradual Civilization Act of 1857*. This Act was really designed to limit Native participation in the rich markets of York, to restrict hunting and gathering activities which supplemented farming activity, and to assimilate the Native population. The response of Native people was immediate. Grand Councils of Ojibway met across Ontario and the Chiefs rejected the *Act* as an act of cultural war. Progress in the areas of agriculture, education, and social and economic development noticeably slowed at this time, and it seemed as though Native people were consciously adopting a strategy of marginalization as a cultural defense, a strategy that has continued to this day.

After the Mississaugas moved their community to the new reserve near the present-day location of Hagersville, Native people continued to travel and trade in the Toronto area and there is some evidence that many Native families remained in the area. However, with increasingly limited opportunity, many of these families occupied a only marginal place in the life of the colony. While there is further evidence of small Native communities continuing to exist in the northern part of the Greater Toronto area, much more research is required to substantiate this. The proximity of many reserves to Toronto and the development of Toronto as a centre of government, commerce, trade and education meant that Native people from communities such as Six Nations continued to exert some influence within the life of Toronto.

Some residents like Dr. Peter Martin (Oryonhyateka) and Frederick Loft had an immense impact upon not only the life of their communities but also upon the development of the city. Dr. Peter Martin was a physician born in 1841 at the Six Nations Reserve. He was educated at Kenyon College in Ohio and earned a medical degree at the University of Toronto in 1864 (with a brief stint at Oxford University). Oronhyatekha became a noted philanthropist as the Supreme Chief Ranger of the Independent Order of Foresters (IOF). The Martin family moved to Toronto in 1883 and lived in a house North of what is now Allen Gardens in the Church and Carlton Streets area. Dr. Oronhyatekha saw insurance as an essential bulwark against poverty and misfortune and concentrated much of his efforts towards convincing others of this. In one story, related by oral testimony, a man from Walpole Island recounted how his grandmother had taken out life insurance as a result of being convinced by Dr. Oronhyatekha. This ensured that, upon her death, her children were provided for at a private school and spared the experience of residential school.[28]

Oronhyatekha died in November 1907 in Savannah, Georgia of heart failure and his body lay in state at Massey Hall for three days while thousands of people came to pay tribute to his life. A newspaper recounted his funeral,

20

The Mayor and aldermen, the members of his Executive Council, representatives of the High Courts and a guard of honour of the Royal Foresters led the thousands who waited at the Union Station for his last return to Toronto. His casket was carried on the shoulders of eight Foresters to the waiting funeral carriage. Then was formed a procession, the like of which Toronto has not often looked upon, to escort this great man and illustrious Forester to Massey Hall. There Dr. Oronhyatekha's body was to lie in state. More thousands of citizens of every degree of all ranks lined the streets. The drawn blinds, the bared heads and the sorrowful faces formed a tribute of respect such as is paid to few men in either life or death.[29]

Conclusion

The history of the Toronto area is one in which the Mississaugas and other Native people were integrally involved. Their full knowledge and use of the area and it's rich environmental resources prior to the arrival of Europeans is attested to by the rich archaeological history of the area, by its recounting in the oral testimony, and by the abundance of place names given to various geographical features and areas of Toronto. Many of these names survive in anglicized forms today such as Etobicoke which was A-doo-pe-kog or "the place of the Black Alders."[30] They also had extensive knowledge of the lifeways of other Native peoples across the Americas and enjoyed participation in a rich trading network which stretched from Mexico to James Bay and from the east to the west coasts. Situated as they were, both geographically and with regards to other nations, they were in a unique position to take advantage of new trading opportunities with Europeans. Their participation in the fur trade was buttressed by their control of two key travel routes in the Great Lakes area - the portages to Lake Simcoe and to Georgian Bay.

The Mississaugas remained in control of their lands and dictated the terms of incursion into their lands. This is demonstrated by the Royal Proclamation of 1763 which was a treaty between nations, the Gunshot

Bobiwash

Treaty (dated variously in the late eighteenth century) which dealt with sovereignty over water and consequently travel routes and resources, and by the several wampums that continue to recount the history of early European and First Nations relations in the upper Great Lakes. The nineteenth century was, however, a great century of change, and in that time, pressures of settlement, disease, competition for game, warfare and a concerted campaign by colonial governments to destroy the traditional political alliances of Aboriginal nations resulted in their marginalization in their own lands. This led to the movement of the Mississaugas in the 1850s to the New Credit Reserve in it's present day location near Hagersville. This did not mean that Native people either literally or figuratively disappeared from the landscape. They continued to press for redress of the injustices committed against them throughout the nineteenth century and into the twentieth. Native people continued to live in the Toronto area both as individuals and communities, but they were like a fire that lives under the moss, burning slowly and gently but with little smoke; they were not to re-emerge again in any significant manner until after the Second World War.

Notes
1. William G. Dean, "The Ontario Landscape, circa A.D. 1600," in *Aboriginal Ontario, Historical Perspectives On the First Nations*, eds. Edward S. Rogers and Donald B. Smith. (Toronto: Ontario Historical Series, Dundurn Press, 1994), 4.
2. For a fuller discussion of this see Conrad Heidenreich, *Huronia: A History and Geography of the Huron Indians, 1600-1650*, (Toronto: McLelland & Stewart, 1971).
3. Dean, 7.
4. Enemikeese, *The Indian Chief; An Account of the Labours. Losses, Sufferings and Oppression of Ke-Zig-Ko-E-Ne-Ne (David Sawyer) A Chief of the Ojibeway Indians in Canada West*, ([London (1867)] Toronto: Facsimile Edition Coles Publishing Company, 1974), 9-10.
5. Enemikeese, 14.
6. Edward Benton Benai, *The Mishomis Book, The Voice of the*

22

Ojibway, (St. Paul, Minnesota: Indian Country Press, 1979) 89.

7. James V. Wright, "Before European Contact," in *Aboriginal Ontario: Historic Perspectives On the First Nations*, eds. Edward S. Rogers and Donald B. Smith (Toronto: Ontario Historical Series, Dundurn Press, 1994), 33.

8. See discussion of Pocohantas and John Smith in Frederic W. Gleach, "Controlled Speculation: Interpreting the Saga of Pocahontas and Captain John Smith," in *Reading Beyond Words: Contexts For Native History*, eds. Jennifer S.H. Brown and Elizabeth Vibert (Peterborough, Ontario: Broadview Press, 1996).

9. Royal Commission On Aboriginal People, *Report of the Royal Commission On Aboriginal People, Volume 1, Looking Forward, Looking Back*, (Ottawa: Canada Communications Group Publishing, 1996), 56.

10. Bruce G. Trigger, "The Original Iroquoians: Huron, Petun and Neutral," in *Aboriginal Ontario: Historic Perspectives On the First Nations*, ," eds. Edward S. Rogers and Donald B. Smith, (Toronto: Ontario Historical Series, Dundurn Press, 1994), 45.

11. Mima Kapches, "Life in the Past Lanes: An Archaeological View of Toronto," *Rotunda* (Spring 1987): 19.

12. Kapches, 21.

13. Trigger, 41.

14. Trigger, 51.

15. Royal Commission on Aboriginal Peoples, *Partners in Confederation: Aboriginal Peoples, Self-Government and the Constitution*, (Ottawa: Canada Communication Group - Publishing, 1993), 10.

16. Royal Commission on Aboriginal Peoples, 1993, 13.

17. Royal Commission on Aboriginal Peoples, 1993, 13-14.

18. Royal Commission on Aboriginal Peoples, 1993, 17.

19. Bruce G. Trigger and Gordon M. Day, "Southern Algonquian Middlemen: Algonquin, Nipissing and Ottawa, 1550-1780," in *Aboriginal Ontario: Historic Perspectives On the First Nations*, eds., Edward S. Rogers and Donald B. Smith (Toronto: Ontario Historical Series, Dundurn Press, 1994), 72.

20. Robert J. Surtees, "Land Cessions: 1763-1830," in *Aboriginal Ontario: Historic Perspectives On the First Nations*, eds. Edward S. Rogers and Donald B. Smith, (Toronto: Ontario Historical Series, Dundurn Press, 1994), 106.

21. J. Burrows, "Buried Spirits," *Globe and Mail*, 3 Mar. 1997.

22. Surtees, 111.

23. Surtees, 117.

24. Peter S. Schmalz, *The Ojibwa of Southern Ontario*, (Toronto: University of Toronto Press, 1991), 106.

25. F. Jones, "Historical Toronto - Toronto's coat of arms offers a history lesson," *The Toronto Star*, 20 Mar. 1976: H6.

26. Quoted in Donald Smith, *Sacred Feathers, The Reverend Peter Jones (Kahkewaquonaby) and the Mississauga Indians*, (Toronto: University of Toronto Press, 1987), 224.

27. Colonial Office Records, *Memorial from the Mississauga Indians of New Credit to the Duke of Newcastle*, (C.O.42, Vol. 624, Sept. 17, 1860): 458.

28. Personal communication between the author and David White (Brantford, Ontario, 14 May 1997).

29. As quoted in Ethel B. Monture, *Famous Indians: Brant, Crowfoot, Oronhyatekha*, (Toronto: Clarke, Irwin and Company Ltd., 1960), 157.

30. Donald B. Smith, 1987, 255. (Appendix 3 of this book contains a list of Ojibway place names compiled by the author with the assistance of Basil Johnston).

The Native Canadian Centre of Toronto: The Meeting Place for the Aboriginal Community for 35 Years

〈3〉

Roger Obonsawin and Heather Howard-Bobiwash[1]

The Centre is People

In its thirty-five year history, the Native Canadian Centre of Toronto has been located in three different buildings and has been known by two different names. To the people who have known the "Centre," however, it has been much more than a name or a building. It has been a positive force in maintaining and developing a strong Native cultural identity within Metropolitan Toronto. The growth of the Toronto urban Aboriginal community in this century, and that of the Centre are inseparable in many ways. As this area on the north shore of Lake Ontario has been *Toronto - the Meeting Place* for Aboriginal people since time immemorial, the Centre has also served as a place where people of many diverse First Nations have gathered to share in each other's experiences and work together to develop the Aboriginal community of today. The Centre has also played the role of an ambassador to non-Native people providing a place for people from all backgrounds to learn from Aboriginal people, and work on promoting equitable relationships between Native and non-Native people. More than a name, more than a building, the Centre is people. To understand the growth of the Centre and its role in the development of the urban Aboriginal community in Toronto, it is important to examine the Centre's "roots." These "roots" were carefully nurtured by hundreds of dedicated individuals over the last three and a half decades and the story of the Centre is not complete without hearing from and about some of these people who have contributed to this important history. Their stories having been conscientiously recorded and wherever possible these experiences provide texture to the story of the Native Canadian Centre and the community in Toronto.[2]

The Formative Years of the Centre and the Context of Aboriginal Life in Toronto: 1950-1969

In retracing the origins of the Native Canadian Centre of Toronto, the year 1950 marks an important beginning because that is when a group of Native people began meeting at the Central Y.M.C.A., downtown on College Street. This group founded what was known as first the Friendship Club, later called the Toronto Indian Club which consisted of volunteers who planned and organized social events, cultural activities, and provided some social services to the Native community in Toronto. One of the original founders of the Club, Eleanor (Jamieson) Hill relates her recollections of those early days, in this volume. She recalls the people and the activities of the Club, as well as how even earlier the founders of the Club originally met at social gatherings at her parents' house in the 1920s.

In the early 1950s, it was estimated that only two to three hundred Aboriginal people were known to be living in the city. In retrospect, the numbers may have been much higher in light of the racism Aboriginal people faced in the city and the tendency of many to respond with "invisibility." Some may have attempted to "pass for white" if possible, made to feel ashamed of their Aboriginal heritage. Many others were cut off from their roots through removal to residential schools. For example, as Hettie Sylvester, born on Christian Island, testified,

> Being at residential school for twelve years took away a lot of my culture. I thought I was like everyone else. It wasn't until I left that I realized I was Indian. And it wasn't until the last few years that I began to understand what being Indian means.[3]

Hettie came to Toronto when she was nineteen, in 1940. She got her first job housekeeping and working as a nanny through the YWCA and was an early member of the Toronto Indian Club. She was later a founder of the Centre's Craft Shop, and the Ladies' Auxiliary for which she served as President for more than fifteen years. Hettie, like many Native people during this time, maintained regular contact with their home communities and a few other relatives who lived in the city. But, they were also simultaneously isolated from other Aboriginal people in the city mainly due to the types of employment available to them, working in factories or individual households. While not necessarily organized with other Aboriginal people during this early period, they definitely maintained a sense of their identity becoming key figures in the development of the community. Like Hettie, Lillian McGregor, also an early member of the Indian Club came to the city as a teenager to work as a nanny, and she pursued her education to become a nurse. Lillian's story is reflective of the experiences of many Native women who came to Toronto during the 1940s and earlier,

> Born on the Whitefish Reserve on Birch Island in 1924, Lillian spent her childhood there... During the summers of 1938 and 1939 Lillian worked at a tourist lodge in her area. In 1939, when she had completed the 8th Grade, she was a waitress there. This, she says, helped her to learn more English, and to gain more confidence in herself. This is also when Lillian had the opportunity to become the nanny for a family from Toronto... Not wanting to compromise the importance of getting an education, she, her family, and the Toronto family worked it out so she could complete high school while looking after the children, and doing her housework duties in the evenings and on week-ends.[4]

During the 1940s, many Native women joined in the war efforts as nurses, relief workers, office and factory workers which also brought them to urban areas. Native men volunteered for the armed forces in very large numbers with 1/4 of the men of some reserve populations joining up. Often after their experiences overseas, particularly after being wounded, they returned to cities and ended up staying. Alvin Hagar, originally from the Alderville reserve recalls his return to Toronto to a veterans' hospital after he received some shrapnel in his leg in Belgium, "I had quite a few people come and see me. Some of the people from the reserve were living in Toronto here and they'd come up and visit." After Alvin was released from hospital he worked at several different jobs including on an Imperial Oil tanker that took him to Venezuela and back. He settled in as a worker for Imperial Optical polishing lenses where he stayed for thirty years. Mr. Hagar, most likely representative of many Native people who remained on the periphery of the burgeoning community says he did not maintain much contact with other Native people in the city at that time, although he did attend socials at the "Y". In an interview in 1982, Mr. Hagar said, "I am as at home in the city as on the reserve. Being Ojibway is important to me. I am proud to be called an Indian."[5]

Many Aboriginal people lost their governmental status as "Indians" when they moved to the city because of the discrimination that accompanied enfranchisement which they were often forced to choose when leaving the reserve. To become "full" Canadian citizens, they were forced to give up the treaty and Aboriginal rights of "Indian status" according to the Indian Act which was designed to eliminate Aboriginal people through assimilation. Prior to 1960 Aboriginal people did not have the right to vote, and were essentially considered wards of the State. Aboriginal people who left their reserves to pursue higher education or professional training had to give up their status.

In the post-WW I period, many faced this difficult choice as high unemployment, disease, and poverty on reserves presented migration to the city as one of the only viable options. Those who started their own off-reserve businesses also had to relinquish status, and the intense regulation of reserve life made it virtually impossible for economic development on reserves anyway. Those who traveled out of the country also had their status taken away. For the thousands of Native men and women who joined Canada's armed forces during the Boer War, the two World Wars, the Korean and Vietnam Wars, signing up often meant signing away Indian status. Women who married non-Native men were forced off the reserve, and also denied their status.

This list of the forms of discrimination leveled against Aboriginal people in Canada is not exhaustive, but does consist of some of the more salient issues, especially for urban Aboriginal people. Attempts to redress some of the injustices of the Indian Act have occurred, such as amendments to the Act in 1951 intended to include "Indians" as full citizens, and Bill C-31 passed in 1985 allowing Native women who "married out" and their children to obtain Indian status. However, the Indian Act and the denial of Aboriginal inherent rights are nonetheless still very relevant to urban Aboriginal identity, to the development of the community, and to the policies and philosophy of the Native Canadian Centre.

During the first half of this century, many Aboriginal people in the city may have lost their "status," and may have even appeared to be "invisible," but they did not cease to exist as Aboriginal people. The members of the Indian Club at the "Y" saw a need in the 1950s for the growing Native community to have its own meeting place. They saw it as a place that would help develop a sense of pride amongst the Native community and would reflect a Native cultural presence within Toronto. In the words of one of the founders, Millie Redmond,

> When I first came to Toronto to work in an office, I didn't know any Indian people. Then as I gradually got to know some I decided we needed a club, so I called the "Y" and asked if we could use their facilities. Our big project was to visit Indian and Inuit people in hospital and take them candy, cookies and comics... I was working in court and learned a lot from the other workers and Native people who had been there a long time. Sometimes I would be afraid to get up in front of a certain judge and one of them would nudge me and say, "Go on."[6]

The Club eventually developed a strong foundation for self-determination for urban Aboriginal people in Toronto evident in the words of thanks given by George Albert Schuyler, President in 1964 at the annual banquet and dance,

> Our Club has been at the forefront of progressive causes, when such causes would benefit the community welfare and improve the lives of Indian peoples now living in Toronto. Our members can take justifiable pride in our achievements over the years, for they symbolize the spirit, the solidarity and the determination of the membership of this Club. The North American Indian Club provided leadership and support for what was good and decent and beneficial for the membership and the Indian people in Toronto.[7]

In its formative years, the Centre's development and that of the community paralleled circumstances in other urban centres across the country. Although the members of the Indian Club were responding to immediate and local needs, developments on a national scale were eventually to affect them and draw them into broad national participation. The 1950s were years of changes for Aboriginal people right across Canada. Through the efforts of the Indian-Eskimo Association,[8] representations were made by Aboriginal people for a Special Federal Parliamentary Committee Examining the Status of Indian People in Canada. Walter Curie, who was later a President of the Centre's Board, made a presentation to the Committee. Aboriginal people were really beginning to organize for changes to the racist and unfair policies that dictated their lives, and the deplorable conditions in which many lived on reserves. Many more people began migrating to the cities in search of employment and better opportunities. This migration was particularly visible in the large prairie cities such as Winnipeg and Regina. One response to this urbanization was the establishment of the Coqualeetza Society in British Columbia, in the mid-1950s. This society, the forerunner of the Friendship Centre Movement, set up an office in downtown Vancouver to ensure that people coming to the city would be able to receive appropriate information and services. Following a conference sponsored by the Indian Eskimo Association in Winnipeg on "Indians in the City" a group of Winnipeg citizens visited the Vancouver office and came back with the idea of establishing an Indian and Metis Friendship Centre in downtown Winnipeg. The doors opened to the first Friendship Centre in Canada in 1958.

In 1960 members of the Toronto North American Indian Club initiated discussions with various individuals and groups in Toronto for the purpose of establishing a Centre. Through the efforts of a field officer from the Canadian Department of Citizenship, additional contacts were made with groups such as the Imperial Order of the Daughters of the Empire and with influential citizens of Toronto. On April 4, 1962, the Canadian Indian Centre of Toronto received its Letters Patent of incorporation, and it became the third Friendship Centre in Canada following the lead of Winnipeg and Vancouver. The Centre held its first Board meeting at the home of D. Le M. Carter. Twenty Board members were elected and a seven-member Executive Committee was chosen including Peggy Jennings as President; James Turner, Basil Johnston, and Mrs. John David Eaton as Vice-Presidents; D. Le M. Carter as Treasurer; Elsie Lickers as Secretary; and Mrs. John Lash as Corresponding Secretary. Later that year the Board was expanded from twenty to thirty members; half were Native. The Board set two goals for the first year of operation: to hire staff and to secure a building. Later in 1962, Jim McGuire was hired as the first Executive Director and Delma Capton was hired as a Counselor.

In January 1963, the Canadian Indian Centre rented a house at 603 Church Street near Charles Street and opened its doors with the official opening ceremonies being on March 30th of that year. In attendance at the opening ceremonies were Lieutenant Governor J. Keiller MacKay, Mayor of Toronto Nathan Philips, and the President of the North American Indian Club, Wilfred Pelletier. In the early days of the Centre, funds were provided by the Department of Citizenship with some small assistance from Metropolitan Toronto. These funds were very limited and the Centre had to rely on donations from churches, individuals and foundations as well as its own fund-raising activities. Many of the women who had been involved with the Centre since its infancy at the "Y" formed the first Ladies' Auxiliary, and along with the North American Indian Club conducted fund-raising events to support the Centre.

31

Invitation to the Opening of the Church Street Location of the Canadian Indian Centre of Toronto in 1963.

In order to keep the Centre open in the evenings and on weekends volunteers were recruited and were responsible for providing coffee, a listening ear, and for filling in a daily log book indicating how many visitors dropped by. It was not until October 12, 1963, however, that the first all-day operations were established at the Centre which have continued ever since. The log-book for that first year of operation indicated that more than 6,000 Native people had passed through the Centre. In 1964 a Christmas Card Committee was formed which was successful in selling enough cards to support the Centre for a four month period in 1965. The 1964-65 participation log counted some 10,000 people taking part in various Centre programs, and almost 16,000 for the following year.

A figure so familiar at the Centre that one could almost believe she brought those 16,000 people to the Centre herself is Pat Turner. Her mother Helen Salter was another of the founding members of the North American Indian Club, her husband James Turner was one of the first Vice-Presidents, and Pat was active as a volunteer with the Centre since her early teenagehood. She remembers those early days of the first Centre fondly, "People could come in to the kitchen and make themselves a cup of coffee and just sit and talk. Or some would come in and play the piano. It was such a homey atmosphere."

In spite of a constant struggle for funds between 1963 and 1966, the Board of Directors and the Centre's administration through the help of volunteers were able to undertake a number of activities including a clothing exchange with Northern reserves, a young mothers' group, Native shows, a float in the Grey Cup parade, and Christmas parties for over one hundred children each year.

Casper Solomon who left his Cape Croker home in 1940 recalled the isolation of life in the city, as well as his revelational experiences in those early days at the Centre when he came to teach Ojibway language classes. He and his wife lived in Mississauga where they raised seven children and he worked at an oil refinery. In 1966 he moved to Toronto and came to teach at the Centre where he also served on the Board of Directors for many years,

At first, in those years, I actually wasn't involved with anything at all with my own people. I guess my concern was to be able to make a living and survive, you know. It wasn't until I came to Toronto that I began meeting Indian people and going to the community centre and seeing what I had been missing. That experience came very late in life. It's like there was a gap in my life over a span of years where I wasn't really living.[9]

Talking in your own language makes you feel alright, like it's okay. I don't know whether everybody feels that way about it, but that's why it's important. I think some people should try to understand some of the language or have a little bit of knowledge of what the language is, even if they can't speak it fluently. You sort of have that feeling of intimacy which you can't have anywhere else. You realize that you are unique in this world. You can identify yourself.[10]

In addition to activities, the Centre also established much needed social services for the rapidly expanding Native population migrating to Toronto. These services included hospital visitation, courtwork services, alcohol abuse counseling, housing assistance, and welcoming newcomers. For 1966, the Centre records show that 325 individuals were aided in attending Magistrates courts, 542 received counseling at the Centre, and more than 2,300 young people had participated in recreational programs which included a gym-and-swim program at Harbord Collegiate, and hockey, baseball, and tennis. At this stage, the Centre served primarily as a referral agency, and had undertaken work with thirty-five other social service agencies in the city to provide access to services for Aboriginal people. The Centre also worked in contact with eighty-nine reserves in Ontario, Canada, and the US. to help newcomers orient themselves upon their arrival in Toronto.

The Centre quickly outgrew its facilities on Church Street and the Board once again set some immediate priorities: to purchase a building to house the growing programs and staff, and to develop a more stable source of funds. Through sizable donations from individual Toronto citizens such as Mr. and Mrs. Sheppard, and Mrs. John David Eaton, the Centre was able to purchase a three-storey house at 210 Beverley Street and took up residence there in March of 1966. On November 26 of that year, almost four years after its first opening, the Centre held a second official opening ceremony at its new location. It was also during this year that the Centre joined the United Way and began to receive funds from the agency in 1967. For the first time it could be said that the Centre had firmly established itself as a credible and growing organization and a recognized agency within Metropolitan Toronto. That recognition was only possible as a result of the tireless efforts of the agencies, organizations, churches, and especially the volunteers who worked together towards this achievement. A bright light among them was Fred Wheatley who taught Ojibway language classes beginning in 1964. He reflected on his participation in helping the Centre during these years of intensive growth,

> I remember scraping off 100 garbage bags full of wallpaper when cleaning out 210 Beverley Street. We had a lot of fun though. It was all Indian people and I could speak Indian again. Young people and young parents are the important ones to be learning the Ojibway language. I'd like to use socializing to teach Ojibway. It's also important for them to know their history. Teaching and being with the youth is very important. The Native Canadian Centre has been my pet project from the beginning. This Centre has been very necessary in Toronto.[11]

With the new and larger location and its expanded funding base the Centre undertook new activities with increased visibility. It truly did become a meeting place in the city of Toronto with a newly renovated library and craft sales room, a monthly newspaper the Toronto Native Times, a volunteer Speakers' Bureau, and participation in the Metro International Caravan. While it was strongly advocated that the Centre remain a referral agency serving as a "bridge" for Native people to access the city's pre-existing

210 Beverley Street location of the Canadian Indian Centre.

services, it soon became apparent that the growing Native community would best be served through Aboriginal-specific services delivered directly from the Centre. A key problem identified with the referral role was the lack of possibility to follow-up on individual cases and therefore the difficulty in assessing and ensuring the services received by Aboriginal people in the city. At the Beverley Street location, the Centre expanded its counseling services to include housing, employment, and child welfare, and established the Legal Advice Centre in conjunction with the Union of Ontario Indians providing court-workers and other legal services. All of these programs eventually grew into separate Native community organizations which are still operating and expanding in the city now. Over time the Centre has clearly demonstrated that Aboriginal control over the design and delivery of social services has best served Aboriginal people in the city by creating the culturally-specific structures necessary to the autonomy and economic development of the community.

On the national front, during the 1960s, Centres began to be established in numerous Canadian cities from Ontario westward. In an effort to provide opportunities for an interchange of ideas among the emerging Friendship Centres, the Indian Eskimo Association and the University of Saskatoon jointly sponsored yearly conferences for representatives from these centres. It was at these meetings that the idea for the National Association of Friendship Centres (NAFC) was formed and a Steering Committee was founded. Victor Peltier, Program Director of the Toronto Centre was named to that committee along with Xavier Michon of Thunder Bay, and Andrew Bear Robe of Calgary. There was some hesitance over the formation of the national organization because many saw a need to form provincial associations first, a move that was taken first in Alberta.

In Ontario, representatives of the Toronto Centre were instrumental in forming the Ontario Federation of Indian Friendship Centres (OFIFC). The NAFC was not officially formed until 1971. In Toronto in 1969, an unpublished research paper entitled "Indians in the City" prepared by the Union of Ontario Indians estimated the Toronto Native population to be 15,000 with a growth rate of 1,500 per year. Under these circumstances the Native Concerned Citizens Committee was formed to begin to define the needs of the Toronto Native community and to look at ways of addressing those needs. Out of these efforts came the establishment of the Wigwamen Housing Corp., Ahbenoojeyug the Native Children's Program, the Native Inmate Visitation Program (Project Reach Out), and Pedahbun Lodge. The increased organization of the Native community in Toronto echoed the consciousness-raising of Native people across Canada and in the United States. In 1969 the American Indian Movement's occupation of Alcatraz Island in the San Francisco Bay gained international attention and added to the momentum of social actions, blockades, and civil disobedience already being undertaken by Native people and their supporters across the continent. Many Canadian Aboriginal people made the pilgrimage to Alcatraz to join in the nineteen-month long occupation. That year, of course, the Canadian government released its White Paper on Indian Policy which was another of many attempts intended to "bring civilization" to Aboriginal people. The White Paper called for an end to Indian "special status" in order to bring Native people to an "equal" level with the rest of Canadians.

The White Paper was immediately exposed for the deceptive tool that it was for the federal government to attempt to rescind its legal responsibilities and obligations to Aboriginal people entrenched in the treaties signed with First Nations. Aboriginal people responded with massive protest, including "the Red Paper" presented to Prime Minister Pierre Trudeau by the Indian Chiefs of Alberta, and the B.C. Indian Position Paper coined "the Brown Paper." These documents clearly outlined the damaging effects the proposed policy changes would have on Aboriginal rights, culture, economic development, and education.

In 1971, the minister of Indian Affairs, Jean Chretien, retracted the White Paper. Well-known "Urban Elder" Vern Harper who was born in Toronto in 1936 recalled,

> Just the fact that people questioned the White Paper and looked at the Red Paper, the whole thing changed. Many people in the Church and the Government realized they had made a mistake; that you can't make a Mistawasis a Jones, and that it's criminal to do it. And there were government people who because of the Red Paper realized they were dealing with sovereign nations and should be treated that way.[12]

Verna Patronella Johnston who ran boarding houses for Native girls working and attending school in Toronto during the 1960s recalled the sense of the "Indian awakening" during these times. In her biography published in 1976, she articulated how the experience of coming to the city, and the need to establish a sense of Native identity and community contributed to both individual and to the stimulation of collective consciousness,

'I grew as a person in those ten years, and I don't mean just running the house for Indian students. I came into contact with Indians from other parts of Ontario, and other provinces. I found out that there were a lot of Indians working to help their own people. All the doors opened now *because* I was Indian.'... Verna says today that what she got caught up in was the upswing of Indian consciousness. Indians were getting it all together, putting themselves forward to get public attention for their rights and their needs, and to work out ways to get what they wanted

(...). She was on the board of the Indian Friendship Centre [Native Canadian Centre] for a long time and that place did good work, helping Indians find places to live, putting on special recreation programs for them, getting them help from lawyers when they were in trouble with the law. 'That is Indians helping Indians — it's not the same as white do-gooders! Indians who have lived in the city know what it's all about, they are the best ones to help people. That place always has been great for Indian people. City Indians had really good ideas about how to help their people adjust to city life.'[13]

Meanwhile, in 1969 the Indian Eskimo Association and the University of Saskatoon announced they would no longer sponsor the annual conferences for urban Centres since they felt their role was no longer required. A year later, with the assistance of the University Women's Club and the Province of Ontario, the Centre organized the national conference at York University. At that meeting the three-person Steering Committee was dissolved and a five-person interim board was elected with one representative from each of the five provinces in attendance. The interim board was given the mandate to begin the process of incorporating the national organization, and the following year in 1971, at the national meeting in Edmonton the

NAFC was officially founded and its first executive elected. Roger Obonsawin was elected as the first President of the NAFC. At both the national and the local levels, the foundations of urban Aboriginal communities were now well-entrenched through the sophistication of organizations like the Centre and the establishment of the national association. However, these structures had grown up rapidly and while it was an exciting time, there was also some trepidation about whether they would bear up under the pressures of the challenges ahead in the next decades.

1970 - 1983

At the turn of the decade, two major issues that had been surfacing over the last few years came to a head for the Centre. The first issue was related to the need for Native people to become more involved in the decision-making and administration of the Centre. The second concerned the need to develop a balance between the provision of direct social services and the development of a community centre serving a broad cross-section of the Toronto Native community. These issues often led strong discussions at meetings, particularly the annual general meetings.

Through the years, the Board had grown from thirty to fifty members. The Board recognized that fifty people constituted too large a number for efficient decision-making and reduced the numbers to twenty-one at the Annual General Meeting held on September 22, 1971. The Board was again reduced to sixteen, in 1974. In 1971, the Centre also introduced its membership plan to raise funds and promote more participation in its programs. In February of 1972, the Centre's name was officially changed to the Native Canadian Centre of Toronto, and that same year it was realized that the Centre had again outgrown its facilities. A building committee under the chairmanship of Clare Brant was set up to search for new facilities. As the size of the permanent Native community grew in Toronto to an estimated 25,000 people, so did the need for facilities to accommodate large social, recreational, and cultural activities. In particular, the Native Children's Program Ahbenoojeyug was established with the hope of operating out of the Centre. It was quickly realized, however, that the Centre's facilities were inadequate to do so.

After a three year search, the Ontario Bible College at 10-16 Spadina Road was purchased as a joint venture between Wigwamen Housing Corporation, and the Native Canadian Centre of Toronto. This was a major gamble by both organizations. A capital fund-raising campaign was launched that included local fund-raising within the Native community and a corporate and public campaign chaired by Russell Merifield of Victoria and Grey Trust. *Project Tah-ran-to* outlined a three-building complex to include the new quarters for the Native Centre, a 120-unit senior citizens' apartment building, and a Native library and resource centre. Proposals were submitted to the provincial and the federal governments, and funds were raised from the sale of the Beverley Street location. Through this campaign, the Centre was able to raise approximately one million dollars, of which $50,000 came directly from the donations within the Toronto Native community. Indeed, the project was highly successful with the new Native Centre facilities holding its third grand opening in 1976, and the Wigwamen Terrace housing complex next door to the Centre, opened in 1978. With the expansion, refreshed goals of the Centre included increased understanding between Native and Non-Native people, programs and activities for all age groups in the Toronto Native community to help in adjusting to an urban way of life, and increased programs of a cultural nature to help develop Native artists and craftsmen, and to aid individuals in retaining their heritage and identity.

In the 1970s, many at the Centre worked hard to encourage pride in Native identity, and to provide information and rally support for causes such as the occupations at Wounded Knee South Dakota, and the James Bay Cree's battles with Hydro Quebec. The Toronto Native Times took on the national media, the justice system, and any others who promoted negative stereotypes and racism toward Aboriginal people. The Centre's newspaper also published as many traditional stories as possible and profiles of leaders in the community and in the history of Native North America.

The Centre also continued to be quite active in the NAFC and the OFIFC during the 1970s, especially in lobbying for increased funding for Friendship Centres. A major accomplishment in this area was the establishment of the Migrating Native Peoples Program through the Department of the Secretary of State in 1972. Unfortunately, by the early

Obonsawin & Howard-Bobiwash

Celebrating the opening of the 16 Spadina Road location of the Centre in 1976.

1980s, the struggles that had been faced by the Centre at the local level in the 1970s between taking the direction of providing social services and that of being a cultural centre were also being echoed at the national level.

After ten years of participation in the OFIFC and the NAFC, the Native Canadian Centre of Toronto, along with the St. Catherines, Thunder Bay, and Red Lake centres, officially withdrew from the OFIFC over the disagreement on the direction being taken regarding the Migrating Native Peoples Program. It had been recommended that the Program be changed to the "Friendship Centre Program" with a narrow focus on social service, rather than broader community development which would include cultural and educational programs, as well as social services — the direction the Toronto Centre had taken. In accordance with this decision, the following NAFC conference passed a motion which effectively prevented any further participation by the Centre in the NAFC unless it resolved differences with the OFIFC. And, indeed, the Migrating Native Peoples Program was changed to the Friendship Centre Program. The Centre continued to receive funding from this program, and was later reinstated as an independent member of the NAFC and remains so today. As the 1970s came to a close, the Centre had to turn its attention to local issues and concentrate on developing a strong urban Native community within the city of Toronto.

On June 23, 1980, the Native Centre was successful in retiring the mortgage when part of the property, 10 Spadina Road, was sold to the Toronto Public Library. This branch continues to house one of the most extensive Native collections in the city. These years saw unprecedented growth in the Centre's operation and budget. At the time of its 20th anniversary in 1983, the Centre was offering such a broad variety of social, cultural, recreational, and educational services that it has since been unmatched. These services attempted to meet the demands of Native people in Toronto of all ages and all Nations, and were divided into two parts: counseling services and programs.

The Centre's counseling services were staffed by a social worker, a satellite worker, a family worker, court workers, a Native inmate liaison worker, an addictions counselor, an employment counselor, an employment outreach worker, and an information and referral counselor. Most of these services are currently no longer available at the Centre as many of them evolved into independent agencies, or government-funded positions were cut-back. Key community outreach positions including the membership and volunteer coordinator, and the information and referral worker were lost in the Fall of 1996 for example.

An important role played by the Centre over the years has been that of providing the non-Native community with speakers to discuss traditional and contemporary issues of concern to Native people. The Centre's Speakers' Bureau was also very extensive at this time, and it does continue to function as a tool to break down the stereotypes about Native people and create links of cooperation between Native and non-Native peoples.

In addition to its social services arm, by 1983 the Centre was also providing a wide array of programs based on the traditional teachings of the circle, as well as a balance of recreational activities. The Centre's roster of programs included drumming, dancing, arts and crafts, Native language classes, euchre parties, coffee houses, and volleyball for the adult community, and extensive youth, after-school, and pre-school programs. Special events were hosted throughout the year such as the Christmas program, summer camps, regular Elders' gatherings and feasts, and two massive fund-raising national Native art auctions were presented at Casa Loma in 1983 and 1984.

In the early 1980s another important feature of the Centre was the development of the Craft Shop run by the Ladies Auxiliary who had been organizing Native craft sales since the mid-1960s for fund-raising. Hettie Sylvester, a key figure in the origins of the Craft Shop told of her involvement,

> I was an organizer. I wanted to do something more every day, every month I wanted to organize something different. When I got to be the president [of the Ladies Auxiliary] I was the busiest person. There was a project going on every month; buying Indian crafts was one. We only sold them on special occasions because we didn't have the space on Beverley Street. Then when we came to 16 Spadina Road, we carried on the same way until the director asked us if

we would like to have the room that was empty. So I asked
the girls, 'Are we going to take that room?' and they said
'Well, give us a try.' And I've been working at it since, as
a volunteer. A lot of people come to me — they take me as
a mother, I think. They come talk to me, tell me about their
problems. But it's good, I liked it. I enjoy talking to these
people.[14]

As the Centre grew, more sophisticated methods for decision-making
and for administration were required to alleviate the strains on both the
Board and the staff. These strains, while leading to increased developments
within the Centre, also led to some loss of community involvement and
participation at a time when other Native organizations were being established
in Toronto. The Centre struggled to cope with the pressures of running
expanded operations and of rapidly changing community needs.

In order to address these changes, the Centre initiated a Family Needs
Study and worked with other Native agencies to establish the Native Inter-
Agency Council. The Family Needs Study identified a number of concerns
felt by the Native community, and the Centre's Board and staff began to
develop initiatives based on the findings of the study. For example, in the
area of business development, the Centre established an economic
development committee which expanded into an independent corporation
with some ties to the Native Centre. The Native Economic Development
Corporation's purposes were to facilitate the development of Native-owned-
and-operated businesses, and to open up possibilities to provide funds to
the Native Centre through the profits. These non-governmental funds would
allow the Centre some freedom from governmental control and restrictions,
and for a greater degree of self-sufficiency, with decisions about the Centre's
funding being determined by the Native community. The Corporation
reviewed business proposals that included a Native restaurant, a travel
agency, real estate development, a major crafts outlet, and a distribution
centre for Native produce.

However, at the close of 1983, in spite of the tremendous efforts to
respond to the rapidly changing needs of the community, these attempts

were not enough. The Centre gradually saw its community base being eroded with a decreasing membership and decreased volunteer and community involvement. It was time for change and re-organization.

Change, Renewal, and Strengthening Our Circle
1984 - 1997

In 1984, the Board of Directors made the difficult and controversial decision to undertake a complete reorganization of the Centre and to place all existing staff on notice. This led to a staff walkout and weeks of demonstrations in front of the Centre as well as a very stormy annual general meeting. Following these demonstrations, and under a new administration, the Centre concentrated on defining its new directions. These included setting the priorities of encouraging the Native community to make greater use of the Centre for social, cultural, and drop-in activities; developing a good information and referral structure, with an advocacy function; becoming a place that reflects a more positive image of Native people to both the Native and non-Native communities; concentrating on Native leadership and development; and ensuring that the Centre reflects a high degree of professionalism in planning, developing and executing activities.

After two years of hard work by dedicated people the Centre was able to rebuild its membership base and its community participation. Two significant achievements during this time included the establishment of an active and involved Elders and Traditional Teachers Advisory Council, and the acceptance by the membership of a new constitution for the Centre, the first major changes since the constitution was initially drafted in 1962. Many of the cultural and recreational programs remained intact, and the Centre concentrated its social service delivery on legal services maintaining a very active court and inmate liaison program. Fred Lamorandiere outlined the goals of this program in 1985, "To ensure the Native people have the best possible representation within the Justice system and to ensure that Native accused and the Native community gain an understanding of the laws, statutes, and procedures that affect them as well as the behaviour that has placed them in the presence of the courts while ensuring that the Justice system is aware of the needs and issues affecting Native people."

In addition, in 1988 the Centre's Legal Services Steering Committee commissioned a study which indicated the high need for culturally relevant legal services. Culturally-specific Native justice initiatives were aimed especially at prevention programs for Native youth, increased services to inmates and ex-offenders, the establishment of sentencing options through the provision of alternatives and the sensitizing of justice personnel to Native needs, issues, and problems, and family stabilization and support to single parents. Eventually, the Centre's legal department also formed into an independent organization, Aboriginal Legal Services of Toronto. By the mid-1980s two other important organizations with roots at the Centre were also established, the Native Men's Residence, and Anishnawbe Health Services.

Bill C-31, aimed at ending discrimination against Native women who lost their Indian status through marriage to non-Natives, or enfranchisement, and their children, passed into law in June of 1985 having a tremendous effect for both reserve and urban Aboriginal populations. The law also amended the Indian Act to strengthen band control of membership. This had both positive and negative effects. The government had widely underestimated the numbers of people who would fall into the category of eligibility for status reinstatement, and this heavily increased pressures on the bands who did not have the financial means to meet the demand. This exacerbated divisions between reserve and off-reserve people, between Native men and women and their national organizations. Anger was unfortunately directed at each other, as well as at the government who were not supplying the support necessary to accommodate the changes to the Act.

The Native Women's Association of Canada had mixed reactions to Bill C-31, warning that while the government had upheld three important principles — the elimination of sexual discrimination, reinstatement of those who lost their rights, and band control of membership — many other provisions caused concern for Aboriginal women. Children of reinstated women would only regain status and not band membership, and leaving membership decisions entirely up to the band councils would exclude the very people for whom the decisions were relevant. These two aspects, they argued, perpetuated further inequalities.

Throughout the 1970s and early 1980s the issue was, of course, central to urban Aboriginal communities across the country. It was in Toronto, that Mary Two-Axe Early originally from Kahnawake, the first woman to regain Indian status under the law, and who had fought the battle since the early 1950s, was presented with written confirmation, on July 15th, 1985. The demand being very high, the Native Centre provided assistance in completing the necessary forms for reinstatement, and the Centre's newsletter reported congratulations on reinstatements well into 1988. Jeanette Corbiere-Lavell who was a youth counselor at the Centre in the late 1960s and who helped the Centre's Youth Group found the Toronto Native Times, gained national notoriety when she protested against being removed from her band membership list at Wikwemikong in 1970 after marrying a non-Native. She maintained that the removal of status from Native women contravened the Canadian Bill of Rights. Jeanette won her case at the Federal Court of Appeal, but the decision was challenged and struck down by the Attorney General's department at the Supreme Court of Canada in 1973. In 1975, Jeanette said,

> Thinking about it now, I still feel it was a victory and worth all the worry and anxiety it produced because now Native people as well as our political Native organizations are looking at the whole question of Indian status and membership. This in itself is one step in the right direction. Changes will have to be made to the Indian Act.[15]

For the Native Centre, the late 1980s also marked the renewal and affirmation of traditional and spiritual teachings and practices. In 1986, the Centre established the Elders and Traditional Teachers Advisory Council who were very active and busy logging in hundreds of hours of appointments with individuals and presiding over feasts and other cultural events. That year, the Centre also held its first Traditional Awareness Gathering, then called the Elders and Traditional Peoples Conference. The theme for the gathering was "Strengthening Our Circle" suggesting the community's desire to strengthen its identity, culture, spirituality, and collective vision.

Janice Longboat, Fran Beaulieu, and Gladys Kidd at the 1989 Elders' Gathering.

These gatherings were held at the Centre at first but needed to move locations to larger premises over the last ten years to accommodate the very large numbers of attendees. Some four hundred people crammed into the Centre for the first one, and attendance now averages about six hundred every year. Ito Peng wrote of the first gathering that it was,

> not just a happy weekend get-together for the spiritual seekers and beautiful people. I heard many serious discussions on the state of our community among the participants. I felt the joy and energy of people singing and dancing together to the heart beat of the drums during the weekend socials. The conference was a circle within which people came together and shared their common humanity. It gave us a chance to learn traditional teachings from the elders and traditional people, and it also addressed some of the most critical issues facing us as Native people in this society today: Native self-government, social injustice and economic problems, alcohol and drug abuse, and our desire for a more renewed community consciousness.[16]

Elders and traditional teachers from across North America are invited to conduct workshops at the Gathering, and many people make very long journeys to attend every year. Held in the Spring, the Gathering provides a sense of renewal to the community and it has really come to be the highlight of the year of the Centre's activities.

Indeed, the Centre continues to serve its dual purpose of ensuring a space for cultural continuity for the Native community, and working on educating the non-Native population on Native issues. In 1988, the membership resolved to incorporate the concept of traditional and cultural programming as an inherent part of all the programming within the Centre. This ensured that all efforts be made to maintain programs such as talking circles and language classes and that staff work and hold their meetings in a traditional way. Cultural activities and events such as naming ceremonies, honour feasts, weddings, and funerals, as well as pot-luck/drum socials have been held regularly at the Centre over the years, and if a few months go by without them it is quickly noticed. The predominant feeling in the community is that the Centre is there first and foremost to provide the place and environment for these social and cultural gatherings. Jimmy Dick who currently coordinates the Centre's cultural programming has frequented the Centre for almost twenty years. He commented on the significance of Aboriginal culture in the urban environment and on the maturation of the Centre's cultural programming over the years,

> After the strike in the early 1980s it took a little while for the people to come back to the Centre. They got a new Executive Director, and then with the establishment of the Elders Council and the Gatherings, with drumming and dancing, and the socials — these were all really good things. But, on the other hand, spiritual practices, like sweats and fasts, were not really emphasized and are still held for the most part outside the Centre. In those earlier times, the problem was that you couldn't get 'too political,' but that was because people had difficulty seeing how the spiritual and political go together.

Jimmy, also a well-known member and founder of the Eagleheart Drum group, spoke from personal experience when he discussed the problem the Centre had in the early 1980s with seeing the inseparable connection between culture and politics. Shortly after the strike, he said Elders were even asked to take the Eagleheart Drum away because of their involvement in political matters such as playing at rallies and protests. Today, however, Jimmy remarked that a lot has changed. The cultural understandings of the people involved have matured and they now see how politics and cultural practices cannot be separated. Jimmy explained the connection between politics and culture, in terms of spirituality,

> When you are spiritually aware, you cannot help but have your political consciousness heightened also. Traditional ways, and doing your ceremonies all the time really heightens your awareness. There

Eagleheart Drummers, 1997. From left to right: Jimmy Dick, Mark Criger, Joe Okitchquo, Sinclair Sabourin, Darrell Gaudreau, Danny Kimewon, Randall May.

becomes no difference between cultural vs. political awareness. Everything you do today has a political consequence, whether you are simply interacting with people, or in the socials. I don't see why you would want to keep that apart — you can't really. They didn't see that having respect is part of the traditional way. It's like these "born-again" Indians, people who get really involved in getting back into the culture and then they go around thinking they can change the whole world from their own point of view. That's what happened with the Drum. It's been thirteen years now, and there has been lots of changes. The people who were dogging us at that time thought they knew a lot actually do know a lot more now and are congratulating the Drummers on their contribution to the community.

In the spirit system, spirits are immortal and can travel for generations and come back in black, yellow, red, or white vessels and people need to be open to that, too — that we are all related somehow, and we all have certain roles and that is a big part of the spirituality. Here, the culture is urban too, and it is very, very strong. We are the advocates here of things going on all over Indian Country. When we are drumming, we are doing more than drumming; we are doing education too. We need to educate not only White people but everybody, Native people, too — the role of that drum, the song, the culture, the contributions by Native people, the issues and concerns, and the promotion of the arts. The Centre goes through phases over time, but the understanding is that its survival — the blood-vein or lifeline of the Centre — *is* the *cultural* component, and that's why the Centre has sustained for so long.

In the 1990s, the Centre has again adjusted its programming to address the needs in the Native community, as well as continuing its role in building relationships with non-Native people. In 1989 a Seniors' Needs Assessment was commissioned by the Centre in which Native seniors identified the requirement for a sense of safety and security, social events such as outings, congregate dining, transportation and accompaniment to appointments, assistance in finding suitable and affordable accommodation, and home help. In January of 1990 the Seniors Project was launched with one staff member and eleven volunteers. The program began activities such as painting, Tai Chi, and beading for the seniors, mainly those living at Wigwamen Terrace. Information sessions on fire safety and tenant's rights were also held that year. The philosophy at the root of the Seniors Program was that in the "traditional perspective" elderly people and children are highly honoured and valued members of the community,

> Developing a program for the Senior segment of the population supported the general thrust of the Centre and enhanced the community in a rich and gentle manner. Community development at the Centre incorporates the theme of self-determination in all their programming and that includes this program for the Seniors. This Program would enable the Seniors to be able to affect their own environments and regain the dignity that is inherent in the original people of this country.[17]

Since then, the Seniors Program has expanded considerably and now includes most of its original objectives, holding congregate dining, outings, bingo, and other activities. In 1996, the Seniors Program employed over ten people and completed its first year of Supportive Housing Services. This service assists and provides support to Seniors so that they can maintain their homes which enables them to stay in the community as long as possible. The sense of independence this provides gives the Seniors security, and the respect and dignity they deserve. Services include laundry, housekeeping, shopping assistance, transportation, help with cooking, friendly visiting, information and referral and accompaniment on appointments.

In 1991 the Centre noted an increase in the number of racially motivated incidents directed against Native people in Canada. The increased profile of Native issues on the national scene following the events in Kahnesetake and Kahnewake in 1990, along with the recessionary economic hardship at this time, and the reluctance Canadians were showing to deal with racism were cited as the reasons for the escalation in racist attacks. In addition, ongoing institutional discrimination in the areas of housing, employment, education, and justice for example, was also seen as a problem the Native Centre had a role to play in addressing. For almost four years, the Centre ran a Race Relations Program which focused on consultation, education, advocacy, and coalition-building. Consultations took place in the Native community concerning perceptions and experiences with racism, and identified anti-racism initiatives.

The Centre also took the lead in educating the public about Native people's experiences with racism and stereotypes; the Centre undertook the great responsibility of the work of "retelling history." In 1992 and 1993, the Centre co-sponsored with the Toronto Mayor's Committee on Community and Race Relations, the Native Community of Toronto Anti-Racism Workshop Series, and produced an Aboriginal Anti-Racism resource document based on the Series. In the area of advocacy, the Centre's Race Relations Program monitored and worked directly with individuals in the Native community who experienced racial discrimination. In 1992 alone, the Program reported 33 separate case studies ranging from police beating to verbal attacks. A great deal of monitoring of the mainstream media was also recorded in the case studies.

Finally, among the many accomplishments of the Race Relations Program was the implementation of the NCCT Anti-Discrimination Policy in 1991 which takes a pro-active stance towards discrimination on the basis of race, ancestry, place of origin, ethnic origin, citizenship, creed, sex, sexual orientation, marital status, family status, or disability. After a great deal of work had been done and many results achieved, the Centre made the decision to deal in part with funding cut-backs by discontinuing this program in 1994.

From the early times of the Native Canadian Centre, the principles of Aboriginal self-determination have been a major factor in the direction and management of the Centre's programs and policies. Even as a budding organization, Fred Wheatley recalled the assertion of Aboriginal control in meetings between the Native and non-Native members,

At our first Board meeting, one of the non-Native people started telling us how to organize things. One guy said he had read a good book about Indian people, so he knew how we should do things. We were all pretty quiet, then Dorothy Jones got up and said something like, "it's wonderful to get up and say what is on your mind. I hope I am not too sharp with my criticism. We want our own halfway house[18] — with your help." At that time we Indians were only something most people had read about in books — we didn't have real feelings and concerns to them. I said that I thought that the dominant society had always had their way. It was time for our chance.[19]

As the Native population of Canada tried to grapple with issues of representation within a constitutional framework in the 1980s, it turned increasingly towards self-government. Aboriginal rights were recognized within the Canadian Constitution Act and since that time Native people have turned to the courts to help define these rights. Urban Aboriginal people were for the most part left out of this process by national and provincial Native political organizations in spite of the fact that in 1992, the Royal Commission on Aboriginal Peoples revealed that 73% of all Aboriginal people in Canada lived off-reserve.

During the 1990s, the Centre saw the flourishing of self-determining sentiment among urban Aboriginal people into concrete plans and strategies. In 1991, the Centre formed the Self-Government Committee which produced the very popular Urban Self-Government Handbook, and held its first Urban Self-Government meeting with more than 300 people in attendance in the following Spring. Since then, the Centre's Self-Government Initiative has worked with a large number of other Aboriginal organizations in the city to develop models and plan strategies. This has included the formation of the Peoples Aboriginal Council of Toronto (PACT) in 1996 with the hope of stimulating the widest possible participation of Aboriginal people living in Toronto (which is, in fact, the largest constituency of Aboriginal people in the country) in self-government initiatives, through the election of a council of representatives to advocate on their behalf and voice the concerns of the community.

In this last decade, the Centre also provided a number of other programs and was involved in many other projects that deserve mention. These include the Disabled Aboriginal Persons Project, the Native Elders Abuse Program, the Aboriginal Employment Counseling and Careers Planning Program, the Aboriginal JobLINK Program, participation in the organization of the 3rd Canadian Conference on HIV/AIDS and Related Issues in Aboriginal Communities, and participation in hearings for the Royal Commission on Aboriginal Peoples, to name a few.

And for the Seventh Generation...

The Native Canadian Centre of Toronto has met many challenges and has overcome many obstacles in its thirty-five years of operation. Most notably it has been able to maintain a healthy balance between ensuring the provision of social services for a growing Native community while establishing a strong sense of Aboriginal cultural identity in the city. The Centre has been able to do so by adopting new and modern methods for addressing social issues facing Native people while maintaining and strengthening its ties to its roots. In maintaining this balance it has exhibited the leadership necessary to preserve Native cultural identity in Canada while helping Native people adjust to a changing and often hostile environment. The challenge is just beginning, however, and the accomplishments of the last thirty-five years should only be seen as the laying of a solid foundation for the future of Native people in Toronto and in Canada.

Notes

1. An earlier version of this article was researched and written by Roger Obonsawin and appeared in the 1987 Special 25th Anniversary Issue of *Boozhoo Magazine* published by the Native Canadian Centre of Toronto. This version has been further researched and updated by Heather Howard-Bobiwash. Special Thanks to Jimmy Dick for his advice and comments on several drafts of this article.

2. In writing this article it is recognized that numerous individuals were

instrumental in establishing and setting the direction for the Centre but have not been mentioned here by name. Those who are mentioned are cited mostly for the insight of their experiences which may be reflective of those of the many unmentioned members of the community, and is not meant to diminish the roles of those who are omitted. We recognize their substantial contribution to the Centre and to the Native community in Toronto.

3 . "Mourning the Loss of Hettie Sylvester," *the Native Canadian Newsletter* (Toronto: Native Canadian Centre of Toronto, Vol. 10, No. 7, 1997): 3. Originally quoted in "Hedy Sylvester: The Founder of the Centre's Craft Shop," *Boozhoo* (Toronto: Native Canadian Centre of Toronto, Vol. 1, No. 4, 1987): 35.

4. "'There's So Much to Learn Each Day' A Profile of Lillian McGregor," *the Native Canadian Newsletter*, (Toronto: Native Canadian Centre of Toronto, Vol. 10, No. 1, 1996): 1.

5. Alvin Hager in an interview with Ranald Thurgood, Native Canadian Oral History Project, tape #OHT82002, Spadina Rd. Library, Toronto, 1982.

6. Secretary of State, *Speaking Together, Canada's Native Women*, (Ottawa: 1975), 108.

7. North American Indian Club, *Program 13th Annual Banquet and Dance*, (1964). In the late 1950s, the Club changed its name again from Toronto Indian Club, to the North American Indian Club. The Club continued to exist into the 1970s and was housed in the facilities of the Centre.

8. The Indian Eskimo Association later became the Canadian Association in Solidarity with Native People (CASNP).

9. Casper Solomon in an interview with Jocelyn Keeshig, Native Canadian Oral History Project, tape #IHOT001A, Spadina Rd. Library, Toronto, 1982.

10. Duke Redbird, "Mr. Casper Solomon," *Dimensions*, (Toronto: Ontario Metis and Non-status Indian Association, Vol. 8, No. 5, Oct/Nov., 1978).

11. "Teaching Ojibway: A Conversation With Fred Wheatley," *Boozhoo* (Toronto: Native Canadian Centre of Toronto, Vol. 1, No. 4, 1987): 41.

12. Vern Harper in a interview with Alex Cywink, Native Canadian Oral History Project, tape #OHT83031, Spadina Rd. Library, Toronto, 1983.

13. Rosamund Vanderburg, *I Am Nokomis Too: The Biography of Verna Patronella Johnston,* (Don Mills, Ont.: The General Publishing Company, 1976), 122, 141.

14. Hettie Sylvester in an interview with Jamie Lee, , <u>Native Canadian Oral History Project</u>, tape #OHT82020, Spadina Rd. Library, Toronto, 1982.

15. Secretary of State, *Speaking Together, Canada's Native Women,* (Ottawa: 1975), 74.

16. Ito Peng, "Update of the Centre's First Elder's Conference." *Native Canadian Centre of Toronto Newsletter,* (April, 1987), 3.

17. Bill Lee, Lee Consultants. *Report on Senior's Needs Assessment for the Native Canadian Centre of Toronto,* (1989), 2-3.

18. By this Dorothy was referring to the Centre as a transitional house for people coming to the city from rural life.

19. "Teaching Ojibway: A Conversation With Fred Wheatley," *Boozhoo* (Toronto: Native Canadian Centre of Toronto, Vol. 1, No. 4, 1987), 41.

My Recollections of the "Indian Club"

Eleanor Hill
with Lorraine Le Camp

In the pre-war years of the 1920s and 1930s, Eleanor Hill's parents Minnie and George Jamieson welcomed Native people into their home on Bleeker Street, north of Carlton. The Jamiesons, themselves young parents of four children, provided a welcoming informal environment for Native people to gather and socialize. Of the frequent visitors to the Jamiesons, Eleanor remembers Mrs. Millie (White) Redmond, Mrs. Ella (Green) Rush, Mrs. Emily (Donald) Sharette (Lorraine Le Camp's mother), Louise Oliver and her sister Hilda Hill, Margaret Wilson, Danny Vet, Oliver Smith and many others. At the time, these people were young and single and had come to Toronto for work and education. Emily Donald and Oliver Smith were attending Normal School, Ella Green was training to be a nurse and Millie White was employed by the Independent Order of Foresters[1].

Both women and men were the recipients of the Jamiesons' hospitality and when the men's lacrosse team from Six Nations would come into Toronto to play they would often be overnight guests. The Jamieson children would bunk down on the livingroom floor in order to give up their beds for the visitors. Some of the young visitors to the Jamiesons, such as Emily Donald and Millie Redmond, were orphaned as young children and grew up in institutional care. Without close family and friends they often found it difficult to establish friendships in a strange, bustling city. Millie never forgot the help she received and came to recognize the needs of others. The early experiences of friendship she found at the Jamiesons influenced Millie's activities and they eventually led to the founding of the Native Canadian Centre of Toronto. What follows are the recollections of Mrs. Eleanor Hill, one of the young children in that friendly house on Bleeker Street.

Lorraine Le Camp

60

In the beginning the meetings of the newly-formed *Indian Friendship Club*, as we called it, were held for a couple of months at Millie Redmond's home on Woodmount Avenue in the east end of Toronto. The following people are those I remember who were in attendance at that time: Margaret Ball, Eliza (Bearfoot) Kneller, Maryrose Kneller, Millie Redmond, Ella Rush, and Emily Sharette. Besides myself and Maryrose (Kneller) Barefoot Jones, the rest of the founding members are deceased. The original group was formed around 1950 by Millie Redmond who was originally from Walpole Island. Her reason for doing so was that she thought a friendship centre was needed where Native people coming into the big city could meet and feel comfortable.

By the fall of 1950 the *Indian Friendship Club* meetings were being held every Friday night at the central Toronto Y.M.C.A. building on College Street. In order to do this we had to have a certain number of paid-up "Y" members. Some of the men actually joined twice in order to meet this commitment. The people at the Y.M.C.A. were very helpful; one of their representatives attended each meeting. The three men I remember were Douglas Drew, Art Stinson and Ted Sexsmith. They told us what was available to us through the "Y" such as a meeting room, the use of the auditorium and copy machine, and they contributed their ideas.

Soon we had increased our membership to approximately 35 members. Other members I remember are Jasper Hill (also known as Chief White Owl) and his wife Kay, the King family including Mrs. King as well as Beverly, Wanita, Gerald and Lorne, Fred Wheatly and his two daughters Gloria and Connie, Bill Blackbird, Mrs. Cameron, Kay and Tom Adams, Helen Salter and her daughter Patricia (Turner), Marjory Hill, Lila Greenberg, Victor Pelltier, Mrs. Antone and her son, Mr. and Mrs. Andrews, Mary Commanda, Delores VanEvery, Doris Kado, Elliott Hill, and Danny Umprevill. There were others I have, unfortunately, forgotten.

Our first committee convened with Jasper Hill as President, Millie Redmond as Vice-President, myself as Secretary-Treasurer, and Maryrose Kneller in the position of Program Convener. The first item on our agenda was to write our "Laws and Constitution" which caused a lot of constructive arguing. We did accomplish these things as Jasper Hill was one who wanted things done right. He saw to it that the Club was formally registered and it was at this time that we changed the name from the *Friendship Club* to the *Toronto Indian Club*. As part of our commitments we agreed to make monthly visits to the *Western Sanitarium* in Weston as there were several Native people there undergoing treatment. Most of these people were from the north and many of them were Inuit. We were able to take oranges, apples, nuts, candy, cigarettes and tobacco in to them twice a year - at Easter and at Christmas-time. The budget for these items came from our Club fees and a few donations. We also held Christmas parties for the children while at the "Y" and we held a couple of banquets in May of the years 1952 and 1953. Most Friday nights were spent dancing to records, playing cards, or just chatting with each other.

Elliott Hill and I met at the Club when it was held at the "Y" and we married in June, 1955. We were the first couple to meet and marry as a result of the Club. We stayed in the city until the Spring of 1956 and left for two years. Upon our return in the Spring of 1958, the Club had moved out of the "Y" and was relocated in an old warehouse building which I believe was next to the Trinity Church, near the Eaton Annex store. As I was only there a few times I cannot remember much about that place.

In 1962, the *Canadian Indian Centre of Toronto* was incorporated. Our next move, in 1963, was to the east side of Church Street just south of Bloor Street. There was a Grand Opening in the Spring complete with Native dancers. At this point we were open five days a week from Monday to Friday. The members of the Indian Club continued to meet there and we volunteered to keep the Centre open. This is when we hired our first Program Director, Delma Capton from the Six Nations Reserve. She acted in this capacity for approximately two years. Jim McGuire was the first Executive Director and I remember him as being very congenial and liked very much by all. He and Delma visited anyone who was in jail. According to Delma there was one volunteer who was at the Centre daily who should be remembered. Her name was Pat Reichert. The actual building itself had a kitchen and a sitting room on the first floor. All the rooms were very small. The second floor had a small library full of books that had been donated. There was also a small office where we did typing and various business transactions.

We desperately needed money at this point and were told we had to have a typed manuscript to be presented to the government stating why

Mrs. Kenneth Albert, Mrs. Florence Tabobodong (Chief of Parry Island Reserve (Wausausking), Chief Kenneth Albert (Chippewas of the Thames at Munsey) at the opening of the 603 Church Street location of the first Canadian Indian Centre of Toronto, 1963. (Photo obtained from Imperial Order of the Daughters of the Empire, Echoes magazine, Summer, 1963, p. 18).

we needed the Centre and what sort of agenda we would have. This would have cost about $3,000 and we had no money. I do not know if this action was ever undertaken, and it was at this time that John Eaton donated a substantial sum of money to us to help pay for our new building. Peggy Jennings along with her friends Mr. & Mrs. Shepherd, and their friends at the Imperial Order of the Daughters of the Empire (IODE) worked very hard on our behalf to help raise money. Mrs. Jennings was always an inspiration to all of us.

Our next move was to Beverley Street and from this point on we were open seven days a week including evenings, and were kept busy with people coming and going. As there was more space in the new building, we were able to have a pool table on the main floor. The sitting room also had a television (which not many people had in their homes in those days). It was here that we formed the Ladies Auxiliary, and were given the use of the top floor of the new building. We often held bazaars and bake-sales to raise money, and we held rummage sales with the clothes that were donated by various people. Wool was donated by the IODE so we were able to knit many articles for sale, too. We also had Native crafts for sale on a small scale and Hettie Sylvester was in charge of this department. We sold boxes of Christmas cards; the first year children were depicted in Native dress, one of a little girl and the other a young boy. The cards were great sellers and we found that we ran short. I resigned from the Board and left the Centre in the early 1970s due to personal reasons and do not know what happened after that time. I hope you find this information interesting and useful,

Mrs. Eleanor Hill

Note
1. The Independent Order of Foresters is a non-profit fraternal benefits society. Famous Mohawk doctor Oronhyatekha was an early "Supreme First Ranger" (1881-1907) of the IOF who advocated for women to join the IOF and encouraged Native people to purchase insurance to secure their futures. Millie was one who benefited from the philosophy instilled in the organization by Dr. Oronhyatekha (Trudy Nicks, "Dr. Oronhyatekha's History Lesson: Reading Museum Collections as Texts," In *Reading Beyond Words*, Jennifer S. H. Brown and Elizabeth Vibert, eds., Peterborough: Broadview Press, 1996).

The Individual is the Community, The Community is the World: First Nations Elders Talk About Education

Suzanne Stiegelbauer

I have to be part of what the young know today, I have to teach them. But the children are teaching us too. They tell us what they need. We need to listen.

Winona Arriaga, Ojibway Elder

We must support our children. We must care for them, make them feel wanted. We must give them their culture, for it is rightfully theirs. It is so important that our children be with our people while growing up. We have lost so many in the past... we cannot afford to lose any more.

Ann Jock, Mohawk Elder

The word "education" has come to mean many things: from the education that children receive in school to the education that is part of being a member of any society or community. Good "education" is successful at both agendas. As such it is "preparation for life" and what life requires, from a set of skills to a sense of personal strength and identity.

This kind of "education" is common to all cultures and all times, even when there were no formal schools. Over time it has taken many forms, from schools to modeling, storytelling and being sent to live for a time with respected aunts, uncles and grandparents — but the goal remains the same — the transmission of cultural information and the preparation of individuals to take a responsible part in everyday society.

Education has also been a part of the mandate of the Native Canadian Centre of Toronto. As of 1986, the Centre revised its objectives to include the formation of an Advisory Council of Elders and Traditional Teachers as part of its governing body to, "help and guide in protecting, preserving and exercising our Aboriginal culture and to promote harmony and common good among our members." The 10 people initially invited to be a part of the Council were nominated on the basis of their reputation as Elders and Teachers, involvement with community, and ability to travel to the Centre (most are residents of Ontario reserves, or live in Toronto). As members of the Council, these Elders were asked to act as counselors to individuals, give workshops on traditional teachings, visit prisons, attend Centre functions as community members, work with Centre staff to develop "culturally appropriate" approaches to activities, and advise as necessary on matters of interest to the Board and leadership of the Centre.[1]

The Elders now involved with the Centre are representative of the First Nations of the Ontario area, as well as from other parts of North America. As the Centre has worked to incorporate more Elders, they became an increasingly important group in facilitating the learning of children and adults alike, about their Native roots and traditions, about how to relate to one another, and about being good members of Aboriginal communities, whether on the reserve or in the city.[2]

Elders' Views of Relating to Youth

As part of Centre planning, Elders have been asked to comment on the many different aspects of what the Centre does. Working with young people was one topic of interest to them and it came up frequently in conversation.[3] As each individual took a different approach to the topic, the following presents some common themes related to working with youth. Where possible these themes are illustrated with quotes from the discussion.

1) *It is the responsibility of the young to learn and the old to teach, both need help:*

As individuals follow the path of life, their needs change. For young people, they have a responsibility to themselves and others to learn what is necessary to live well. During the early years of their life they are taken care of by others so that they will have the freedom to do this. In adulthood, they will use these skills to earn a livelihood for their families. As older people, they have a responsibility to communicate what they have learned back to the young so that the circle is completed. While learning is a life-long process and teaching often a matter of example, in general each characterizes the states common to the opposite ends of the path of life.

Both the young and the old need help in order to complete their work well. The young need the help of structured situations where they are exposed to what they need to learn. In a traditional context this would be done through becoming a "helper" to an Elder or teacher so that they learn through discussion and example. The old often need physical help, the help of directed questions (the young need to ask), and the help of good listening, respect and interest. In helping the Elder, the young create the opportunity for new experiences and guidance. Youth also need to ask their Elders for help to set the process of knowledge in motion. Ojibway Elder Gladys Kidd said,

> *We have watched our young people, you know, growing up and so on and we've wanted to help them, but you can't go to the young person and say, Hey, I'd like to help you. It has to be the other way around because when they ask you it becomes the "given." You have then an obligation to share what you can. So that's the process.*

2) *The young need to know who they are:*

Perhaps the most persistent theme in discussions with the Elders is the importance of knowing who one is, as a Native person. So much of Native lifeways has been lost to history that often what is left is coloured by negative stereotypes, separation from a positive sense of community, poverty and social distress. The Elders felt strongly that young people need to be re-educated about who they are so that they can positively identify with it.

They need to know more about the values, traditions, strengths, and history of their people. Developing strength in who they are and understanding something of a traditional framework for viewing the world helps them consolidate the fragmented information they may have about their culture in terms of contact with other cultures, and gives them a framework for choices. Knowledge of who they are often comes through enhancing or maintaining Native language skills. Elder Art Solomon made this comment,

> *Native people feel that they have lost something and they want it back. It doesn't necessarily mean that when I talk about going back over there, that we stay over there. You have to get those teachings and pick up those things that we left along the way. The drums, the language, the songs are all scattered around. We need to bring them into this time. You need these things to teach your children today in order to give them that direction and good feeling about who they are. They need to know where they are going. It doesn't mean we have to go back to living in teepees. You can be a traditionalist and be comfortable wherever you are.*

3) *Discipline is necessary but so is understanding the reasons for discipline:*

Young people should be respectful of those older than they, if only

68

because they know more having gone further on the path of life. When they are told to do something, they need to respect those in authority and do it. Such discipline is a part of learning. However, they should also be instructed in the reason for following directions, or the reason for the learning. Ann Jock, a Mohawk Elder, talked about her own children,

When a person has the right directions and the right bringing-up they can't help but be that good person. Good discipline is very important. One of the most disciplined things is when a child is a child, he grows up to respect the Elders, or anybody older than him. He never talks back. When he is told to do something, he is to do it without saying "no, I don't want to." When my oldest son was graduating from high school, I asked him to get a pail of water. We lived on a farm and did not have running water. He said, "No, Ma, let David do it." He's getting ready to go to graduation. I told him, "I brought you kids up and I told you never talk back to your parents. When you're asked to do it, just do it." He grabbed the pail and went out of the room and in about a minute he was back with the pail of water. He said, "Ma, you surprised me because I'm graduating tonight and I thought I wouldn't have to get the water." I said, "It's just the way you talk back that I didn't like. When you're asked to do your share of the work, you just do it and get it done with." He was sorry for a whole week. If kids don't know about respect you have to start to explain how that (getting water) has to be done and how water is so important to the cooking and it's so important to wash up with water, the cooking, the medicine. If someone got sick, we need that water there, so that's why it's important that it be there. What is the water for? To quench our thirst, you always talk about what that is. It is

> *important to take time to explain to a child. The*
> *understanding, the caring is always there. They*
> *understand how... from grandparents and all, aunts*
> *and uncles, that love and communication was all*
> *strength there. Nobody hollered at them, but they*
> *knew.*

Having water in the house there helps maintain the quality of life for all. The child's responsibility is to do their share to that goal as directed by those older, especially older relatives. Doing this is a part of learning to be a community member and learning what is necessary to support life as an adult.

4) Schools offer skills that can contribute to the good life; there is no necessary conflict with traditional lifeways:

The Elders were concerned that Native people often felt they had to make a choice between their traditional life and beliefs, and what they learn in school, particularly since schools have been a vehicle for the assimilation of Native students into mainstream society, forcing them to give up their culture, often with negative consequences. The Elders expressed that now the world has changed in a way that makes it necessary to seek a balance between the knowledge available through learning to read, write, and become competent in mainstream culture, and that knowledge available through traditional skills.

Tradition provides a base for knowing "who you are" and for acquiring the values contributing to a healthy Native community. Schools (and other things available in the modern world) offer tools that can contribute to life as an adult, providing means for work and personal growth. Ojibway Elder and Traditional Teacher Jim Dumont describes how a relative of his helped him understand the meaning of life tools, whatever their origin,

> *As a child I went to residential school for a few years.*
> *I hated it so much I would not use English when I*

went home. I would always speak Ojibway. One day I was helping some seniors build a boat. I was using a hammer someone had bought at a store. A regular hammer. One of the Elders asked me what was that tool I was using. I said, "a hammer." They said, "Where did you get it?" I told them I got it at the white man's store. They said, "Does it do the job? Why can't you use English like that?" They helped me see that I could use it as one tool to do what I had to do in life.

In a similar vein, Eddie Benton-Benai made this statement,

There is no teaching against being comfortable. No teaching against accumulating things that are good for your family or yourself. I sit in the lodge and I sing songs and I fast and go to the sweatlodge. Sitting in my house I play the guitar and the banjo. I love baseball. Young people think these things don't work together. Of course they do. But how can they know without someone to tell them, to show them how to live successfully. More and more of the people out there are waking up and returning to the lodge. Not giving up the other things, but heeding the call. In that lies the hope for our people and the world.

5) *Youth are a part of the community, a part of the whole:*
As Gladys Kidd stated,

In the Native community, all children are welcomed, regardless of where they come from or who their parents are. Each one is respected, right from birth. Everyone in the community is responsible for the children. If a child cannot be with his/her parents, then it is up to the community to help that child grow up strong.

Too often in the last generation, children have been left without guidance. The Elders see that guidance as the responsibility of the community, in part to help them grow as community members. In the modern context, people often have to work hard to find and form communities to develop that kind of sharing. The activities of the Native Canadian Centre in Toronto have attempted to replicate some of the dynamics of a traditional community, especially those related to social gatherings, teachings, access to Elders, and training for new skills. Communities can be created. In the view of the Elders, however, one important function of community relates to educating the young in their cultures and providing support and guidance for working within other cultures.

Education and the Path of Life

> In general, the Elders and traditional teachers perceived and defined community from an organic, relational perspective. Their vision of community can be characterized by three dominant features: 1) an extension of self and family; 2) a gathering of individuals with a shared, spiritual history and cultural understanding; and 3) an evolving entity moving toward some form of wholeness or relatedness, often expressed in terms of a circle.[4]

The Elders' comments about relating to youth are based on their experience and on traditional concepts of how children develop into adults and what is important to that path of development. One of the roles of the Elders within the Native Centre has been to teach about traditional concepts from First Nations perspectives. As part of a Centre community project, two Ojibway traditional teachers, Jim Dumont and Dorothy Christian presented the basis for individual and community growth in their discussion of the *Path of Life*, the path that all people follow in their individual ways as they progress through life.[5]

Figure A: The Path of Life [6]

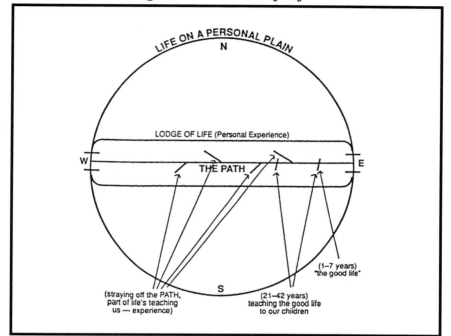

The *Path of Life* begins in the east where the sun rises and moves through the years and through seven major stages to the west (see Figure A). As individuals follow their own path they have many experiences; some are based on their age and where that age fits on the path, others are individual, contingent on what life has presented to them. Elders consider these factors in individual and general terms when offering guidance to people who come to them. Jim Dumont talked about it this way,

> *When we walk this path, we carry with us all we have learned and are about to learn. We may walk this path as individuals, but we are never alone. We experience with others and learn from others. How we interpret and make use of this learning is called experience. How we learn from our experience and use it in a good way is called wisdom.*

73

On our *Path of Life* we meet up with seven stages, the first of these, representing early childhood is the period of discovery of *the good life* which is a fundamental guiding principle for the rest of life. During this, time the foundation is laid for later learning through the experiences parents and other adults provide for us. Children have the instinct and need to explore for themselves. At this point, however, they have little real responsibility. This is a time of giving and safety. Life should be easy,

> *When we are born we are taught to walk the "path" by our parents. This starts for all of us, ideally, when we are between the age of one and seven years. During this time in our life we learn and want to experience for ourselves. We are taught by our parents and Elders. They steer us toward the "path" and give us their experience, the best of what they have gained through their lives is offered to us.*

The second stage is roughly the time between age seven and puberty. During this time children take on more responsibility, gathering teachers and support for learning. This is the time to try things out with guidance. At the end of this phase, in some traditions, girls and boys may go on a vision quest to help further determine who they are as individuals. The next phase, the teenage years, is one of rebellion and testing where the forces of sexuality and physicality create strife for young people. During this time they begin to go their own way and to seek other kinds of teachers. They share more together as peers. This phase may last until the individual is in their early twenties and is a time of seeking and solidifying the truth of their individual selves. It can be called a wandering and wondering stage.

During the next phase, representing the years of adulthood to age 45 or so, the individual begins to show evidence of what they have learned, to form and support a family, and to take on concrete responsibilities in society. A number of the Elders commented that individuals have often not accumulated enough experience to speak and give opinions at community gatherings until in their mid-thirties. These first four stages involve responding to what life presents, to gather experience and knowledge.

The last three phases of the *Path* represent what an individual makes of what they have learned, what they have to offer themselves and their community. During the mid-life years, an individual experiences a process of "letting go." A number of the Elders called this a powerful time, a time when women and men are more alike and when family responsibilities lessen.

The next phase is that of the teacher and grandmother or grandfather. People begin to seek you out for what you have learned and the guidance you have to offer. The last stage continues this progression of age, but in an even deeper sense. While often winding down many physical activites, Elders in most Native cultures remain very active as teachers until the end of their lives. Since interactivity is the key principle underlying the teacher-learner relationship, however, Elders need to keep being engaged by the members of the community who rely on their guidance until the end of life. At this point, it is the responsibility of the community to value and care for individual Elders in the community. A person at the end of life is closest to the spirit world, as is the young child, but with the wisdom of life experience. As an Elder, one has the opportunity to be a beacon for others.

Elder Gladys Kidd stated that there are two basic principles of *living the good life*. The first is to grow in our own life and spirit; the second is to share life with others, to be "helpers to everyone and everything," all people and all creation. Actions taken in life are both for the benefit of our own lives and the life of the people. The seven stages of life are often represented on the *Path* as "seven stones," or important moments given to each individual in which to learn fundamental teachings. An important aspect of understanding how to approach these teaching stages is in gaining perspective on the significance of the individual in the community in terms of how one's actions effects future generations. It is often said that with our actions come the responsibilities of their effects on seven generations to follow.

75

Stiegelbauer

The Relevance of Experience

While the ideas presented in the *Path of Life* relate to seven general stages and kinds of experience, not everyone has the same experience even if in the same stage. Elders Fred Wheatley, Art Solomon, Jim Mason, and Ernie Benedict spent a lot of time with people in prisons, for example, and Fred related,

> *All our personal paths are not straight. They take their turns and sometimes we stay at these turns and twists until something we gain from experience tells us to walk the "path" again.*

This reinforces the idea that experience in itself is an important teacher. Even if people had experiences that are difficult for them, with the help of Elders and family, they can return to a healthy path. This is, in fact, more the norm than not having difficulties occur. Many of the Elders on the Centre's Council have talked about how they fell off the path, or suffered other difficulties that made *the good life* difficult to maintain. Because of this, they feel they can offer guidance to others to get back on that path. As Art Solomon described,

> *The Elder knows where the land is solid. He has been on that other path and found the way back to the good one. He can help others get there.*

If individuals have had a good foundation in the early years, or good guidance, they will naturally seek to return to the good way. The path and its benefits will attract them as a matter of health. It is also a matter of human nature to wander from it. However, it is the responsibility of individuals to in some way understand and monitor how far from the good way they are. It is the responsibility of teachers and the community to help them understand this. Many of the comments of Elders about children and education are based on the concepts of having good foundations, discipline,

Figure B: Medcine Wheel [7]

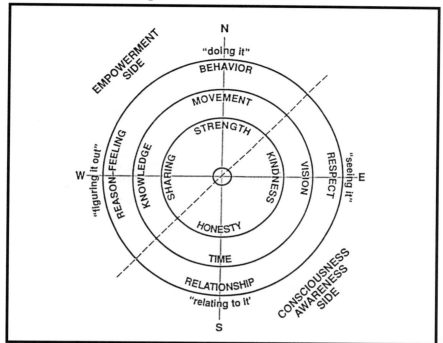

and guidance, and the understanding that each person has their own experiences to live. As they do, they learn that they need to also have something to offer future generations.

Qualities of individual action and growth: the Medicine Wheel

Another life teaching tool used in a number of Native traditions is the *Medicine Wheel.* The word "medicine" conventionally means "that which contributes to health." Figure B represents just one version of how different Elders or teachers may present *Medicine Wheel* teachings. The circle of the *Medicine Wheel* adds another dimension to the path of life in that it is constantly turning around that path as in a spiral, presenting different values and attributes of behavior to individuals as they grow and mature.

The qualities expressed in the *Medicine Wheel* emphasize that people depend on each other and have a responsibility to themselves and each other. The ideal person one aspires to embodies the qualities *of kindness, honesty, sharing, strength, vision, respect, reason* and *feeling* in their everyday actions and in their relationships with others, all represented in the *Wheel*. In theory, individual and community health occurs when these qualities are put into action. When we have respect for ourselves and others, we treat each other more carefully.

Understanding the relationships one person or element has with another helps us to see how they might work together or be interdependent. Reason and feeling are the key to knowledge in that true knowledge is the attempt to understand the meaning of *vision*, through both the heart and the mind simultaneously. Finally, the end product of this is expressed through behavior: people become what they have learned.

How an individual learns about these things, including how to accomplish a vision and gain knowledge and experience is also represented in the *Medicine Wheel* is divided into four quadrants: *seeing, relating, figuring it out, and doing it*, all parts of a process. Imbedded in that process are the indicators of how this process should be embarked upon: with respect, with feeling, allowing experience and relating to develop over time, through sharing and kindness, and developing knowledge from all these factors. It portrays action, behavior, and strength or confidence as the result of the process and as contributing to growth through the process in an ongoing way. The emphasis on vision is also an emphasis on individual talents and a human need for meaning.

The *Medicine Wheel* and the *Path of Life* describe learning as continuous and integrated, with different emphases at different points in life. Learning is interdependent with other parts of the whole. It is not linear and separated from everyday life, but acts on everyday life as experience is accumulated. It is a process that starts with the self and develops through interaction and choices.

The tie between the community and the individual is a reciprocal one; because the community survives it nurtures the individual, as the individual is stronger, the community is stronger. Writer Basil Johnston discusses this relationship in the Ojibway tradition, *"the more resourceful the individual, the more whole, the more strong, the better for his community."*[8] The Elders emphasize the need to strengthen individuals in order to strengthen the community. As one Elder said, "A whole person is one who is strong in spirit, body and mind living in necessary coexistence with others."[9]

The individual is the community, the community is the world

For the Elders, the dynamic relationship between the individual, the community and the world is one that provides a capacity for constant regeneration and renewal as part of an ongoing, organic process. Most importantly, it is a collaborative process where the parts inform the whole and vice-versa, where the young and the old must participate together in order to build upon the past and survive the future. The relationship between the individual, the community and these potentially changing circumstances, is one grounded in tradition and traditional values but sustained by communication and dialogue. It is not static. As people interact about who they are in a new circumstance, that circumstance is transformed to express that relationship, that belonging, and becomes a part of their past and present as a "people." This in turn, strengthens individuals' concepts of who they are and why they are here, as Aboriginal persons, and as healthy human beings.

The involvement of the Elders Council at the Native Centre is an attempt to provide access to traditional teachings with the outcome of strengthening Native people, and the Native community in the city. What the Elders have to say comes from the perspective of living in the world as it is today, and considering the concerns and issues facing Native people. People strong in their identity are more able to cope with the pressures of whatever society they choose to live in. The Elders talk about the role of community, about responsibility, about what is natural to life, about helping each other, and about rediscovering self through tradition. They see the community as a dynamic being with "a life cycle; it has good and bad elements; it experiences both sickness and health, just like any human being."[10]

The Elders see working with individuals and working with the community as one and the same thing. They emphasize the need to strengthen individuals in order to strengthen the community. This is where the idea of education comes in again, not as an academic process found only in schools, but as a community process that is an interactive preparation for life. From the perspective of these Elders, education means constant learning through life's experiences and through the guidance and wisdom of the Elders. This learning is learning through body, mind and spirit, it is multidimensional (as the *Path of Life* and the *Medicine Wheel* describe) and it is always happening. To keep education as a process on its own "good path" requires more than the right curriculum; it requires considering the whole person.

According to the Elders, as healthy individuals and healthy communities are formed, and as people begin to understand and act on their relationships within a community system, they will in turn begin to understand their relationships and responsibilities to the world. Therefore, the individual is the community and the community is the world. As one person becomes healthy, other positive relationships will fall into place. As the world stands now, this is something worthy of working for.

Acknowledgements

The information presented here is part of the ongoing work of the Native Canadian Centre of Toronto Board of Directors, the community, and the Elders who have given so graciously of their time and energy. Elders' comments and information presented from Board workshops are meant to be available for everyone's learning, and hopefully are presented accurately. The writer and the NCCT wish to say Chi Meegwetch to Barbra Nahwegahbo, Gayle Mason, Martin John and the staff over the years, as well as all the Elders and Traditional Teachers involved with the Centre through the years, some of whom have passed on but who have left us with a tremendous legacy: Thom Alcoze, Winona Arriaga, Mary Assiniwe, Josephine Beaucage, Ernie Benedict, Eddie Benton Benai,

Shawani Campbell Star, Dorothy Christian, Jim Dumont, Vern Harper, Ann Jock, Verna Johnson-Sylvester, Roger Jones, Gladys Kidd, Brad Kiwenzie, Isabelle Knockwood, Janice Longboat, Willie MacLeod, Edna Manitowabi, Lillian McGregor, Jim Mason, Herb Nabigon, Betty Pamp, Angus Pontiac, Isaac Pitawanakwat, Tom Porter, Helen Salter, Pauline Shirt, Paul Skanks, Sarah Smith, Art Solomon, Hettie Sylvester, Joe Sylvester, Jake Thomas, Ella Waukey, Fred Wheatly, Jim Windigo.

Notes

1. Suzanne Stiegelbauer, *The Road Back to the Future: Tradition and the Involvement of Elders at the Native Canadian Centre of Toronto*, PhD Dissertation, (Austin: University of Texas, Austin, 1990).
2. Suzanne Stiegelbauer, "Who Are Elders? What Do They Do? First Nations Elders as Teachers in Culture-Based Organizations." Canadian Journal of Native Studies (Brandon, Man.: Fall, 1996).
3. Ito Peng, *Minobimadiziwin: An Examination of Aboriginal Paradigm on Community and its Policy Implications*, (Hamilton, Ont.: Unpublished Master's Thesis, McMaster University, Hamilton, 1990).
4. Peng, 31-32.
5. James Dumont, and Dorothy Christian, *Board Development Workshop*, (Toronto: Native Canadian Centre of Toronto, 1988).
6. James Dumont, *Ways and Means Committee*, (Toronto: Native Canadian Centre of Toronto, 1988).
7. Dumont, 1988. For more on the teachings of the Medicine Wheel in Anishinawbe tradition (Ojibway, Odawa, Pottawatomi), see Ernestine Buswa and Jean Shawana, eds. *Nishnaabe Bimaadziwin Kinoomaawinan; Teachings of the Medicine Wheel*. (Ojibwe Cultural Foundation, West Bay, Ontario, and N'da Gkenjge Gamig, Wikwemikong, Ontario, 1992).
8. Basil Johnston, *Ojibway Heritage*, (Toronto: McClelland and Stewart, 1976), 70.
9. Stiegelbauer, 1990, 312.
10. Peng, 66.

Elders' Ideas on Growth and Learning

*The Elders at the Native Canadian Centre in Toronto
describe learners, and reciprocally
working with learners, as having the following
characteristics, as the Path of Life and Medicine Wheel
teachings suggest:*

1) The foundation for the "good life" or health and capacity for learning is modeled through the structure and behavior at home during the early years.

2) As a child develops in age they can be asked to take on practical responsibilities relevant to their age. These responsibilities go beyond tasks to values, gathering experience, understanding it and expressing it in behavior. This changes developmentally as a child ages. Learning is a life long process but each stage has different qualities. Learning involves mind, body and spirit simultaneously not separately.

3) Experience is the foundation for learning. Understanding experience is developed over time through dialogue. Experience is neither good nor bad but a natural result of exploration.

4) Children should be allowed to make choices and to gather unique and individual experience within the framework of modeled values, discussion and community good. Each individual has something unique to offer as a result of who they are and their accumulated experience.

5) Learning is a process that is accomplished through interaction with others; it is always a shared, cooperative venture.

6) The foundation for interaction with others is expressed through respect, feeling, a good heart, good intentions, kindness, sharing and a knowledge of self.

7) Each individual is unique yet a part of a whole community. The community and the individual have reciprocal responsibilities. In one sense the individual and the community and the world are the same entity, interdependent. What affects one, affects the others.

8) Learning begins with vision — of self, of goals, of the whole, of the direction a task is to go in. It is a process that goes through the stages of "seeing" (vision), relating to what it is, figuring it out with heart and mind, and acting on findings in some way (behavior).

9) The old and the young need each other: one to provide the understanding of experience from their own experiences; the other to frame that discussion in terms of current and changing needs. The child's world may be different from that of the adult as it reflects a changing world.

10) Everyone has a responsibility to give back and to consider their actions in the light of their effect on generations to come.

Native Urban Self-Government in Toronto and the Politics of Self-Determination

A. Rodney Bobiwash

Across the globe Indigenous people are engaged in a radical demographic shift from largely rural land-based communities to large urban centres. In Canada, this trend began in the 1930s and has since steadily increased. Today 73% of all Aboriginal people in Canada live off-reserve; in Ontario this includes 55% of all "status-Indian" people. This has created a number of challenges for both Aboriginal peoples as individuals who are often ill-prepared for the rigours of urban life, and for Aboriginal collectivities overwhelmed by the stresses of meeting the rapidly growing and changing needs of Aboriginal people not confined to reserve territories. These challenges are compounded by local, provincial and federal authorities who lack both the political will and the necessary human resources and social services infrastructures to meet the needs of Aboriginal people in cities.

In Toronto, it is accepted that there are approximately 65,000 Native people living in the city. However, this estimate acknowledges the difficulty in counting actual numbers without being able to account for the people who have recently moved, the numbers of occupants in a household, or street people, for example. Unlike the western cities such as Winnipeg, Saskatoon, Regina or Edmonton (all of which have large and visible Aboriginal populations) Native people in Toronto are conspicuous by their anonymity. Although there are some pockets of the city where there appears to be greater concentrations of Native people, such as where the Gabriel Dumont non-profit housing complex is in Scarborough, or in some parts of the downtown core where Native street people are more visible, there are no Native neighbourhoods, or specific areas of Toronto which have become "Indianized" in the same sense that there is a "Chinatown" on Spadina, a "Greektown" on the Danforth, or a "Little Italy" on College Street.

The 52 urban agencies that deal with Native people in the city have mostly developed to meet the needs of people in crisis: shelters, health clinics and facilities, alcohol treatment programs, food banks, housing, and other social services are all predicated upon need. They are all a part of a strategy of crisis-intervention which, while necessary, works to marginalize and further disenfranchise the majority of Native people in the city from involvement in civic life and political processes. Torontonians, and Canadians in general, continue to cling to outdated stereotypes of the "urban Indian" as a social problem, much in the same way we were described by Edgar Dosman in the first major work on these issues in the early 1970s.[1] Native people in the city are often stereotyped as the bum at the bus station begging quarters for a drink, or the Native street kid hanging around on the corner, although Aboriginal people in crisis in Toronto represent only about 18% of the total Aboriginal population. This number is still far too high, and the difficulties for these people are compounded by the fact that they often may have many different needs while they are simultaneously discriminated against in multiple ways. The other 82% of Aboriginal people in the city are primarily working-poor who constitute a silent majority within the urban Aboriginal polity. It would be erroneous to believe that because these people are not direct consumers of crisis services, they are not also experiencing high degrees of ethnostress, cultural dislocation and social isolation.

Another issue of concern regarding urban self-government is based in the diversity of the Toronto community. Many Native people living in Toronto maintain a "commuter" lifestyle if their home communities are in close geographical proximity. For example, many people from the Six

Nations of the Grand River, or from Tyendinaga Mohawk Territory (both within an hour and half driving distance) literally commute back and forth either daily or at least on weekends. For many of these people, their cultural, spiritual and mental locus is situated on their First Nations. This means that their views on the need for urban self-government arrangements can be very different from those of people from most Anishnawbe (Mississauga, Ojibway, Chippewa, Odawa, Pottawatomi, Cree) or other communities which are farther away. For those from Anishnawbe communities which are in close proximity (New Credit, or Rama for example) perspectives on self-government are often tied to the land claims of these communities since the actual physical location of the greater Toronto area *is* their traditional territory. It would be interesting to compare, for example, attitudes of Six Nations people living in Vancouver towards urban Native self-government to those of Six Nations people living in Toronto, or the attitudes of Anishnawbe living in Sudbury or Sault Ste. Marie to those of Toronto Anishnawbe.

In any event, regardless of where they come from the majority of Native peoples living in the city are not even acknowledged as existing much less as having any legitimate voice in decisions made which affect them, or having a legitimate voice in decisions affecting the larger urban polity.

Another problem faced by the urban Aboriginal community is the artificial and arbitrary separation of social service provision and political representation. Aboriginal people have always governed themselves by the principle of what is called in Ojibway "Bimaadziwiwin," or the principle of the "good life." Political leadership, the appointment of "Ogimaws" or "bosses," was predicated upon the ability of the Ogimaw to provide the good life to their people. For Native people, a system of governance in which there are two arms -- a civil service and a legislative arm independent of one another -- is usually incompatible with their traditional forms of government. The division of these two functions of governance is being effectively used by the Canadian and provincial governments to deny urban Native peoples, who have only ever organized themselves in the city on the basis of need, the right to political representation. This error, one of the most misunderstood issues regarding urban self-government, is demonstrated again in the conclusions of the recent Report of the Royal Commission on Aboriginal Peoples.

Aboriginal political organizations structured as they are all too often complicit in their involvement in the process of the disenfranchisement of urban Aboriginal people. First Nations limit the right to vote in band elections by residency provisions. Aboriginal political territorial organizations fail to invite urban Aboriginal representatives to gatherings and indeed make no provision for their participation in any decision-making capacity.

They also often compete with urban Aboriginal organizations for program funding, claiming some form of priority enabling them to decide for the majority of Native people how program funds are to be allocated. When asked where this imperative is derived from, they refer back to the inherent Aboriginal right of self-government as though all Aboriginal people had always governed themselves in contemporary political organizations, yet most are less than two decades old.

This, of course, is supported by the federal government which has deliberately worked since 1969 to quietly implement the provisions of the White Paper on Indian Policy, an assimilationist document as patently racist, patronizing, and harmful as the one that spawned it, the Indian Act. By centralizing all Native programs, under the guise of devolution, in the pockets of a few "brown" bureaucracies, the Canadian government will be poised for the final stroke, the divestment of any fiscal, moral, political or historic responsibility for Aboriginal people in this country.

When we discuss self-determination for Aboriginal people in Canada, whether it be a limited form of self-government or sovereignty, we must be aware that there is a large number of Aboriginal people who are left out of the formal equation; the deliberate exclusion of these people is a gross human rights violation. Any form of self-determination which is limited to territorially-defined First Nations communities should therefore be rejected on the grounds of morality. If Aboriginal people living in urban areas are to be included in self-government or self-determination arrangements, the following questions must be asked:

i. Where does the right to self-determination flow from for Aboriginal peoples living in cities as opposed to those still living on First Nations reserve lands?

ii. How is the right to self-determination to be exercised in an urban centre in the absence of a discrete land base?

iii. What are the jurisdictional issues that need to be resolved?

iv. How are urban Aboriginal people to be represented?

In the Toronto case, when the Native Canadian Centre of Toronto first embarked upon the process of defining an urban self-government model during the winter of 1990, there was, in retrospect, some naivete among the Board members and community people who came together to form the first Self-Government Committee. While Native people in the urban milieu agreed on the need for more resources and the need for greater control over those resources, they were divided on the definition and the meaning of self-government. As with any large and diverse community a number of viewpoints were expressed ranging from the desire for a federally-chartered municipal form of self-government (like the Sechelt case in British Columbia) to outright sovereignty. This was not surprising given that the urban Native community has been organized around social service agencies.

At that point the need for an urban self-government model was simply based on the twin factors of the increased need for access and control of resources to serve the urban Aboriginal constituency, and the realization that the self-government bandwagon (the Constitutional train) had passed urban Aboriginal people by, leaving them standing at the station, bags in hand, looking wistfully at the departing locomotive. As the exercise continued it became obvious that the task before the Committee was threefold: 1) Define the issues; 2) Frame the issues in a manner understandable within the community; and 3) Define and seek consensus on an approach to deal with the issues.

The first task seemed relatively easy and could be divided into two areas, issues of governance relating to service delivery, and issues of governance relating to representivity. The process by which these issues were defined was both reactive and proactive. The Committee anticipated that issues such as a stand on the land claim of the Mississaugas of New Credit would be necessary given the geographic location of Toronto in the traditional territory of the Mississauga. To this end they sent letters to then Chief Maurice LaForme in support of the land claim; they drafted a statement to that effect in the Committee's Goals and Objectives; they reiterated support for the land claim in much of the correspondence with municipal and provincial authorities; and they specifically invited representatives of the Mississauga to all public consultation meetings.

Also, when issues identified as having implications or importance for self-government arose in the community, or were brought to the attention of the Committee by a community member, the Committee would take a stand and lobby upon the issue, or send letters to the appropriate authorities. The problem with this approach was that the Committee soon became overwhelmed with issues brought before it, and the internal discipline of the Committee was subverted by people with narrow agendas. Nevertheless, during this time a number of issues arose and were dealt with as self-government issues, particularly those relating to the delivery of services. In this process it became clear that education, health care, legal services and the justice system, child welfare, and housing were self-government issues under the definition of governance as the provision of human services to the people. This approach was in no way revolutionary either from the perspective of the history of the urban aboriginal community of Toronto, or from the perspective of larger self-government negotiations as Aboriginal band councils had been seeking control of these programs and services for years.

There was a presumption, however, that the task of governance was synonymous with the purpose and action of governance. By this I mean that the strategies adopted over the course of many years by Toronto's Aboriginal social service agencies as a means of survival became detrimental to the course of the development of a self-government model. When the bottom line was reduced to how urban self-government will provide a direct human need, the model was driven by considerations for how we will continue to ensure that we get adequate resourcing for our programs and activities. One model that is often pointed to as an example is the Urban Society in Vancouver. Those who are enamoured by this model are quick to point out that the Urban Society controls vast pots of money and distributes them throughout the Vancouver Native community. This is a step forward from the days in which all funding was controlled by non-Native governments, and it is an interesting model for the administration of service dollars, but is it self-government? What has been sadly lacking from the debate is any kind of discussion on deconstruction of the state and traditional structures and ideologies governing the manner in which Native people in urban centres relate to the State in both rhetoric and practice. While some Native writers and thinkers have tried in different contexts to apply a variation of Fanonian analysis in terms of the idea of the "colonized Indian mind," or others on even rarer occasions have articulated some post-colonial and post-modern discourse, this has seldom gone beyond a rationalization by Native people for the continued acceptance of oppression. What is usually posited sounds much like the vision of the Royal Commission On Aboriginal Peoples,

> Our initial research indicates that the inherent right of self-government does exist off a land base, and that, in urban areas, it can be exercised, albeit in a different manner. For example, the right might be exercised through self-governing institutions supported by provincial legislation.[2]

This position exemplifies the *realpolitik* of Native politics in the 1990s. There are many examples of precisely this kind of partial autonomy in some urban contexts. In Toronto, an urban school authority (First Nations School) is maintained under provisions in the provincial Education Act; some Native child welfare agencies (Native Child and Family Services) are given status under provincial child-welfare statutes; and, an alternative

Native justice system (Aboriginal Legal Services of Toronto Community Council Project) is supported by the provincial office of the Solicitor General. There is even recognition on the part of municipal authorities of the need for Native agencies to serve Native people, and this manifests itself primarily through the provision of contracts to urban Native agencies, usually on a fee-for-service basis. It is hard to say that this assertion moves us very far beyond the limited and restraining vision of self-government meaning only greater control and access to resources for programs and services. The only positive aspect of this statement is that in recognizing provincial initiatives in this area it might bring greater pressure to bear upon the need for urban self-government negotiations to be carried out on a tripartite basis, in a tripartite forum. Self-administration is not self-government!

Provincial governments in some provinces appear to be eager to hand over control of Native program and service dollars to Native people. In Saskatchewan the provincial government identified up to $550 million a year in the areas of health, education, justice and social services that could eventually be transferred to band council administrations, Metis groups, and other Native organizations.[3] Provincial governments like those of Saskatchewan and Ontario are fed up with waiting for a Constitutional amendment, they are tired of waiting for a process that will never come about, and are intent upon negotiating bilateral agreements with Native people in their provinces. While this is commendable and a step forward the issue once again is whether the bilateral process allows the federal government too much latitude to shirk their fiduciary obligation to Native people.

The legality of whether provinces even have authority to negotiate agreements with Aboriginal governments is another question. Among the arguments used by the federal government in regards to provision of social services for off-reserve Native people has been that if the provinces are the main beneficiaries of lands and resources under Lands and Resources Transfer Agreements and Acts (by which the provinces also became parties to later treaties such as the Williams Treaty of 1923) then some of those benefits ought to go to support off-reserve Native peoples.

91

Bobiwash

It is an invidious argument which carries on the logic of Section 91 (regarding the division of powers, in the Canadian Constitution) at the same time as it refutes that logic. At any rate, as Aboriginal self-government becomes a reality, the real budgets, the real dollars being vied over by Aboriginal organizations will not be the four billion dollars a year supposedly spent by the federal government on Native people in Canada, but rather the billions spent in provincial funds for Aboriginal social services.

Responsible governance supposes a number of prerequisites, 1) An identified and willing constituency; 2) An informed constituency; 3) A willing and accountable leadership; 4) A Fiscal base; 5) A sense of Nationhood; and 6) In a neo-colonial situation, there must be a willingness on the part of the ruling powers to surrender power and negotiate an orderly transition. There might be those who also add to the list above the need for a territorial imperative, the need to enforce territorial boundaries, and the need for the state to control a legitimate monopoly of violence within the territory. I believe that these concepts are, however, part of an outdated state-based conception of nationhood which has little relevance in the world today, although it still maintains all of the inertia of the status quo.

While states will continue to exist, and will maintain armies, police forces, prisons and other instruments of coercion and violence at their behest, pluralities of citizenship within state boundaries will lead to a necessary redefinition of concepts like citizenship. Already we see within Europe the breaking-down of discreet national boundaries within the European Economic Community; the creation of a common European passport, the lifting of trade barriers between countries within the EEC, and talk of a common currency across Europe must lead to a redefinition of citizenship. If a person can be an Italian yet access employment, medical benefits, welfare, and a host of other social and economic benefits in France, Germany, Belgium or England what benefit remains in Italian citizenship? As the engines of commerce grind on in North America, likewise, under NAFTA and as economic benefits become somewhat harmonized, or rationalized, with a basic level of access to social programs and services for all North Americans, what benefit will remain in maintaining Canadian,

American, or Mexican citizenship? In the creation of this New World Order there is no doubt that further balkanization of nation-states, accompanied by strident nationalism will occur, however, the reasons and the definitions for Nationhood will need to be redefined to reflect this.

It has been said in a paper prepared by Peter Jull for the Royal Commission On Aboriginal Peoples,

> For the nation-state, whether Canada or Norway, governments must now ask themselves whether the old hackneyed responses to indigenous ethno-politics are relevant any longer. That is, the indigenous renaissance is not an old irritant requiring stronger measures from a stern state -- although both Oslo and Ottawa are full of respected people who think so. Rather, it is part of a genuine "new world order" - and one which has little to do with lines in the sand. National capitals and policy makers can either embrace this - as some elements in Canada have been doing with Inuit in particular, and with First Nations and Metis in parts of the north - or lose all credibility. The wilful old men of the Eastern Europe capitals were not the only political dinosaurs in our landscape. The ability of nation-state structures and pretensions to survive will depend upon the capacity of politicians and officials to adapt to the socio-cultural changes which are happening regardless of their preferences.[4]

In the same manner that Chechens, Afghanis, Tajikstans, and other Indigenous peoples of the former Soviet Union were able to exert a powerful influence leading to the break-up of that nation-state, Aboriginal peoples can exert powerful geopolitical forces to influence government policy and state structures in Canada. As Urban Native people find voice and representation within the polity of the country, we also realize that this basic expectation can be fulfilled for us only beyond a series of unfair hurdles and barricades. The process leading to self-government for urban

Aboriginal people will mean we will demand a greater say in the places we live and we will demand not only the same level of service as other Canadians but also recognition as Aboriginal people with Aboriginal rights to be exercised wherever we choose to live within our traditional territories. Governments who ignore this and those who do not anticipate it would do well to look at recent events in Peru, Mexico, New Zealand, and other centres of Indigenous organizing around the globe. Urban Native people in these places have demonstrated that as cities exceed their capacity to care for their citizens those who cannot find voice through legitimate political processes will take up more marginal expressions of political activity. The conviction of Indigenous rights coupled with autonomy of political expression will inevitably result in the disruption of state processes. The question that remains is whether that disruption will eventually lead to a better or a worse society for all who share the city -- for all who share the space on the lands of Indigenous peoples.

Notes:
1. Edgar Dosman, *Indians: the Urban Dilemma*. (Toronto: McLelland & Stewart, 1972).
2. Rene Dussault and Georges Erasmus, "Notes for a Speech...," *Royal Commission On Aboriginal Peoples*, (Toronto, February 1, 1994) 12.
3. "Millions earmarked for natives," *Globe and Mail*, 16 Feb.1994.
4. Peter Jull, "A Thousand Years: Indigenous Peoples and Northern Europeans," *Royal Commission on Aboriginal Peoples*, (June 11, 1993) 15.

Profiles of Our People: Aboriginal Lives in Toronto

Barbara A. Gajic

The profiles in this section provide a glimpse of the lives of people in the Toronto Aboriginal community. The interviews were conducted during the spring of 1997. They are meant to represent the diversity and dynamics of the community through a range of perspectives shared by these individuals who have so kindly and generously agreed to tell us their stories. Women and men of different cultural backgrounds, ages, and professional lives give us their points-of-view on issues of concern to the community such as the importance of language and culture, the politics of the community, and the role of education, and Aboriginal people in society. They tell us of their own personal journeys, how they came to the community, what they found there, and how they see the future.

Life stories are not meant to represent the "worldview" of an entire population such as the urban Native community in Toronto, but they do provide insight into how individuals actively participate in shaping and building that community. They tell us how people understand the social issues of the community, how they interact with these issues on a daily basis, how their own lives are part of the life of the community, and how urban Aboriginal people are integral to the larger picture of world Indigenous histories, politics, and cultures. The people profiled in these next pages have in common an emphasis on the importance of their sense of identity as Aboriginal persons, and of the rich potential of the future of the Aboriginal community in Toronto and all its resources and diversity. We are most grateful to all of these individuals for their contributions to this book, and more importantly to the community. Finally, we extend special acknowledgements to Catherine Grimwade who selflessly gave up countless hours of her time assisting with these profiles.

Gajic

Jim Mason

"The kind of reward you put into your heart"

Most any day of the week you can rely on finding Jim Mason in his "office" or his "pit" as he calls it -- that is the bench outside the Native Canadian Centre where he knows he'll have the opportunity to meet Native people who might be too shy to walk up the intimidating steps of the Centre and go inside. He is there to listen, and to share his experience with all those who are keen to learn. He is not often alone on his bench. There are always people of all ages sharing a story or a laugh with Jim. Recognized as an Elder in our community for some time now, these few pages can hardly do justice to the many enlightening experiences of Jim's life, but even if only a glimpse, we can certainly learn a lot from those parts of Jim's story that he has so generously agreed to share with us here.

Jim Mason often refers to himself as "the beginning of a new breed: the Urban Indian." He was born in the downtown core of Toronto, at King and Peter Streets. His father was from the Six Nations of the Grand River (about 90 kilometres south-west of Toronto) and his mother was Anishnawbe from Rice Lake First Nation (90 km to the east). Jim never knew his parents because as he says, "My father died in March, I was born in April, and my mother died in May." Since his parents left their reserves, under the Indian Act they became enfranchised and were no longer entitled to return to their lands. As Jim explains, there are many Native people in the city who come from these situations; with no roots or property to go back to, they are the "Urban Indians."

Jim was shuffled around between various relatives in the city after his parents died, and by the age of twelve they considered sending him either to work or to residential school. It was at this point that Jim struck out on his own and he remembers these times vividly,

97

> *I was getting to be too much of an expense. They said, "We can't afford to keep him unless he goes out and works or goes to the residential school." I had older brothers and sisters in residential schools. I heard what it was like for them. So, I eavesdropped and I heard they were going to send me to residential school. But, they were going to have to catch me first! I had my pyjamas on. I went back into my bedroom and put my overalls over top of my pyjamas. I took off and I haven't been home since.*

Growing up, Jim never denied his identity as a Native person, but he did have relatives and friends who did. Jim recalls how his brothers and sisters would, "deny they were Indian because they couldn't get a room or a job. I always knew what I was and wasn't ashamed of it." The issue was a source of tension between Jim and his family because they did not want to even talk about the fact they were Native people. Jim remembers how his brother, who was taller and darker than he, would tell everyone he was from Scotland! "He would get mad as hell when they [at work] referred to him as *Indian Bill.*"

Jim's education consisted of the basics, reading and writing, but he did not state where he learned them from. Jim worked at many different jobs from the time he was very young in order to survive. These jobs ranged from picking fruit and vegetables in the Niagara "Golden Horsehoe" region where a lot of Native people worked in the summers, to cutting wood in the bush to be sold by the cord in the cities in the winters, to steel work in many different places in Canada and the U.S. Jim spent a lot of time working in construction, in Hamilton at the Dominion Foundaries and with the National Steel Car company. This is where Jim started to work for the Hamilton Bridge company. He has fond memories of working in construction and steel and how this kind of work became a positive niche for young Native men,

They used to hire right out of the field. They would be lined up and the foreman would come out. If he needed men, he knew them and he knew which ones he wanted. He would ask, "Are you Native? Can you climb." If you said, "Yeh sure." He would say, "Go check into the time office." They would always hire the Native guys. These guys could climb and were dressed for it. They wore overalls rolled up and their belt around it and a big wrench stuck in there. We used to call that their turnkey. It was a good life for young guys because you were all over the country. Hamilton Bridge always put up steel. We would like to get the jobs out of town. If there was a big job in Nova Scotia they would send the boys down there. We got paid for travelling time and board allowance.

It started in Montreal with the Mohawks. They were building the first bridge across the St. Lawrence and that was in the days before night-watchmen and security guards. At night the guys from the reserve were out there climbing the iron like monkeys and even diving off into the water, and the company got worried. If they got hurt or even killed the company would be responsible. So, they thought if those guys can climb like that, put them to work. So they did. When the construction company moved back to New York City, they took the workers with them. Most of the sky scrapers in New York in those days, the steel work was put up by Mohawk Indians. The Indians built these places.

Jim went on to say there were also a lot of the buildings in Toronto that he worked on, and added with a laugh, "They're still standing!"

While working hard all of his life, Jim also found time to get married and raise a family. Jim has four boys and one daughter. Today, Jim says the daughter, who lives in Hamilton, is the boss of the Masons. His sons are Jay, Malcolm, Andy and Tona. When asked if he had any grandchildren, Jim replied, "Who can count that fast?" Jim is very proud of his children and he feels education is very important. He tells his boys that, unlike himself, they went to high school and even a bit of college, and should strive to do better than he did, "and they are!" he adds with delight. Jim said he was always trying to be the best in his work, "No matter if it was iron working or steeple jacking, I wanted to be the best. Maybe I wasn't the best, but I was up there with the top ten."

After working many years in construction, Jim hurt his back and had to quit. For the next 14 years, Jim drove a transport truck for the Canadian Pacific Railroad (CPR). About this time Jim's wife passed away and he took it very hard. He was all alone. The older children were out on their own, and the young ones were with their grandparents. "I went on a big drunk for a while, and when I do things I do them good." After a while, though, Jim stopped drinking and got a job doing maintenance with the Native Centre which was still located on Beverley Street at that time. Jim recalls that most of his life, he felt like he had to compete with everyone. But, once he started to work with other Native people he didn't feel the need to compete anymore,

> *I didn't want to compete with my own people. When I was with the CPR, I quit at five o'clock. If I worked 'til five-thirty, I'd check my pay and if that half hour wasn't on my pay I'd raise hell. I came to work at the Centre and if I got busy doing the floors I put in until eight or nine o'clock before I'd get out of there, and I'd start laughing to myself because I knew, there (at CPR) I'd raise hell about half an hour overtime, but here I am working a twelve- or fourteen-hour day and not even complaining because I'm with my own people. I knew what I was doing it for.*

Jim would never take a day off and was always at the Centre. One time a friend of his boss told him to let Jim have a day off, but his boss replied, "What would be the use; he'd show up here anyhow."

Jim was especially concerned about Native people who chose to leave their homes on the reserve, come to Toronto in search of a better life for their families, and for varying reasons would often get trapped here. In the earlier days, Native people had no place to continue practicing their culture and traditions in the city. Jim felt very strongly that the Native Centre should serve this purpose and is very pleased to see so much activity going on there. Without that cultural activity, he feels the Centre is just another office building.

Jim also worked in the legal services program at the Centre which is where he began the invaluable work he does with inmates in correctional institutions. His work began as an outreach worker but his responsibilities grew and his job expanded. Jim was instrumental in getting this program established which has since become an agency independent of the Native Centre, Aboriginal Legal Services of Toronto. The outreach program consisted mainly of organizing trips to the prisons to bring visitors to inmates. Jim was in charge of the vans and he did a lot of the driving. He eventually became very closely acquainted with the inmates, and helped them to organize themselves to obtain access to the means to participate in Native cultural activities in the prisons.

Jim left Toronto for a while and worked in a similar capacity for the Metis Association, helping inmates in the north. When he returned to Toronto, he came back to work at the Centre, but this time he helped Vera Martin start the Children's Program at the All Saints Church on Dundas Street. Jim's main duty was to pick up the children from their homes and drop them off for the program at the Church. At the Church, in the same office, there was an organization called Springboard. Springboard used to run a bus service from Toronto to Kingston taking people to visit inmates in the penitentiaries there. "At first," Jim said, "I used to avoid them because I thought they were a bunch of cops." But, when his job at the Children's Program ended, he got a call from Doug McCorran who was in charge of Springboard, asking him if wanted a job

101

driving for them. Jim worked for eight years with Springboard before retiring. Jim usually had to wait two or three hours while the passengers he drove to the institutions were visiting with inmates. He took advantage of this time to meet and visit with the Native inmates. Soon Jim was on the visiting lists of each one of those institutions. He said it was like killing two birds with one stones; he had the chance to visit with some of his own people in the prisons, and he could make a living by doing the driving. Even though this was his last job, it was only the beginning for Jim. After he left Springboard, he had even more time to devote to visiting Native inmates in the institutions. After spending so much time working with inmates, Jim can say that the majority of the people in prisons today are there because of drugs or alcohol. Jim has heard many tragic stories about how so many Native men ended up in prisons,

> *They all say, "If it hadn't been for the booze, I wouldn't be here." That's true. They all say that. It's an awful feeling to wake up one morning and you don't know where you are, all you see is bars and the guard going by. You think you're in there for a drunk and then the guard tells you, you wasted a guy last night. All the toughness goes out of you and you just sit on your bed and bawl.*

Jim also feels strongly that residential schools and foster care (Children's Aid Society), both run by Christian churches, are largely responsible for a lot of what has happened to Native people. Jim's views about Christian religion may offend some people, and non-Native people often have difficulty understanding this connection, but there are also many who will agree with him about the damage that has been done to Native people. The destruction of families, and the removal of children from their own cultural environment to one where they are often frightened, abused, and made to feel worthless because they are Native, whether this occured in residential schools or in foster care. It is a devastating experience that often turns people to drugs and alcohol. As Jim says,

Native men in prison want nothing more to do with the white man's religion because of the connection to children's aid and the residential school. In the prison they have a chapel, but they want to see their own people, they want their own Elders, their sweats and drums.

While Jim is happy to visit so many of the Native men in the prisons, responding to their requests for help, he also finds it most unfortunate that they had to go to jail in order to find their way back to their own culture. Jim sees himself acting mostly as a sounding board for these men. Often he does not even have to say much to them at all, just listen, and give them the opportunity to review their lives, see where they went wrong, and how they can move on. Jim remembered one time he had driven some distance to one of the prisons. As soon as he arrived, the first man he saw met him with a barrage of criticism. At first Jim was quite put off by this man's condemnations, but then the man calmed down, apologized, and Jim realized he simply needed to get his frustrations off his chest. Jim is concerned how these men become "institutionalized," and explains how the formation of the *Federated Brotherhood* in federal prisons, and the *Native Sons* in provincial prisons are so important to Native inmates both in terms of providing spiritual guidance inside, and the sense of identity and confidence they need to face the world when they leave the institutions.

I had one guy last summer, in my office out here. He had just gotten out. He had done twelve years. He told me while walking the streets, he was actually scared in the city and wished he was back in prison. Scared to walk across the street, scared to talk to anyone. When your life gets to that point where you're wishing you are back in prison... but that's the way they get. Some of them get right back into the wrong things on the street and others don't. It takes them a long time to get over that prison life. The streets are bound to get you in trouble. Many kids run away from foster care and have no place to go except to the streets. He knows he's Indian because they have told him. He's scared to come to the Indian community because he doesn't know if he's going to be accepted. So he stays on the street and he gets into trouble. On the inside, they are looking for these "new fish," that's what they call them. Once he joins the Brotherhood, he gets acquainted with sweetgrass. He has never seen it before, never heard the drum before, but when they have the social and he hears the drumming, he gets right into it. He knows who he is now. Those guys turn out good. They start going to sweats.

Jim says there are a lot of success stories to tell, too,

One guy I saw in four different institutions. He got out and got a job, and went on from there. One day we were sitting in the restaurant having coffee, and he says, "They get out of jail and are picked up on another charge and go back in. I've got society paid off. They can't pick me up for nothing. I've got my own room, some new clothes, and money in the bank, and a good job." He reached over and slapped me on the back, and he almost knocked me to the floor, and said, "I owe it all to this old bugger here who followed me from one joint to another telling me that I could do it." Now the guy is married, owns two cars and has a family. He's not the only one, there are a lot of others.

At the age of seventy-seven, Jim is a very wise and knowledgeable person who knows a lot about life, because he has lived it. Jim has received many awards for volunteering his time in the community, and says, "My favourite reward is not the kind that you put into your pocket and carry to the bank. It's the kind of reward that you put into your heart and carry to the grave."

In 1992, Jim was presented with the Ontario Medal for Good Citizenship by the Honourable Henry Jackman, Lieutenant Governor of Ontario at that time. Of the six recipients who were chosen out of three hundred, Jim was the only Native person. The plaque he received read, "To recognize the sacrifice for the common good in all areas of our society, and for the outstanding behaviour that is a distinct qualification of a Good Citizen, Jim Mason." After the ceremony, reporters were asking Jim what the highlight of the evening was for him? Was it shaking hands with Mr. Jackman? Not for Jim who replied, "When we came down off the stage and went down into the audience, my son Jay came up to me, put his arms around me and told me `I'm proud of you Dad.' I almost bawled. That was my proudest and most memorable moment, but that never got printed in the paper."

Jim says he is always learning and that an Elder is never too old to learn from young people. In today's society, Jim maintains that an education is important for Native people to be successful but not at the price of losing who we are. These stories from his own life, and from the lives of others like the many Native inmates he has worked with, remind us that pride in our culture as First Nations people is really the key to success.

Bob Crawford

"If you don't meet all the needs of that circle, they're going to break apart..."

Bob Crawford is from the Algonquin Golden Lake First Nation. He is of the Bear Clan, and was recently given his spirit name, "White Eagle" by four elders in the Native community in Toronto where he has lived for about thirty years. The underlying meaning of his name is, "to help the native community and Native people." Bob's story definitely attests to his dedication to this responsibility, having worked for 27 years with the Toronto police force, and now as the Director of Spirit of the People, an organization he formed and has devoted his life to, helping Aboriginal ex-offenders renew their lives when they leave prison.

At the age of three, Bob was left in the care of a Catholic orphanage by his mother, and he never knew his biological father. Over the course of the next 12 years, Bob was shifted between four different foster homes, and at the age of fifteen he decided to strike out on his own. As he recalls,

Being in the foster homes, because it was white homes that I was in, I had to struggle to find out who I was. Having to do all this searching, it's difficult for a young person to go out and find who he is. I can relate to anybody that comes into the Centre here now, in that we've all been victims of that system, of society -- of residential schools, or one thing or another. Everyone of us somehow, somewhere, someway in their lives as Aboriginal people have gone through this. It is a sad story, and one that needs to be told, but there is no need to go into all the details of hardships because we all know them.

Gajic

Against these odds, Bob completed grade 12 on his own, working at various jobs to support himself. He then went on to a secretarial course where he learned bookkeeping and typing which got him a job as a management trainee at Kresge's in Renfrew, Ontario. Bob worked there for four years before he decided to move to Toronto and try to get onto the Toronto police force -- and try he did -- certainly if anything can be learned from Bob's story it is perseverance; it took him three years and eight tries before he finally succeeded. When asked why he was so determined to become a police officer, he replied,

> *I don't know. Well, I do know but I didn't at the time. At that time you had to be 5' 10" tall to be eligible to join the force, and I was a quarter of an inch short. Now, why in the hell did I try eight times -- something compelled me, and now I see that the reason is I can sit here now running Spirit of the People knowing the justice system from A to Z, and this will help my people.*

Bob was the first Aboriginal person to make Sergeant on the force, but he is also the first to say that he finds it unfortunate that there are, in fact, far more Aboriginal police officers, some of whom have also risen in the ranks, who do not wish to acknowledge publicly their Aboriginal heritage, preferring to "pass for white,"

> *There are many police officers in Toronto who won't identify, and that is their right. But, I remember in 1969, going in to the office and saying right up front, 'This is who I am, like it or lump it.' I've always been up-front about who I am. It doesn't work too well to live in two worlds. At one time it used to, but now it doesn't because Aboriginal people have stood up to be recognized for who they are. They're people. And, if you want to make it in this world you have to fight*

108

*for who you are, and keep fighting as you go. I've
done all types of police work from walking the beat,
driving the patrol cars, to undercover work for ten
years. It is not a career I would encourage anybody to
go into.*

Bob has been married for 26 years and has two daughters. His wife
was born in Ireland, and although they are from different cultures, Bob
feels strongly that there is a great deal of support and understanding between them.

*It's quite a diverse home, I guess. My oldest daughter
goes more along with the way I believe and practices
that way. She speaks fluent Ojibway now, even though
she is Algonquin, but there are mainly Ojibways around
here. I have my sacred fire in my backyard, and my
wife supports that. And yet, she also goes to church
on Sundays and does her thing. She respects what I
do, and I respect what she does, and it goes to show
that even though we are very different we can still get
along if everybody would just show enough respect.*

Spirit of the People, Bob explained, is a very unique organization in
all of Canada, but there certainly is a demand for the kind of work they do
to help Aboriginal ex-offenders. Bob recalled how he came to form the
organization in relation to a number of struggles and frustrations with the
treatment of Aboriginal people by the justice system in general,

*I spent 27 years on the police force and through the
justice system I found out that there was a lack of
support for Aboriginal ex-offenders when they came
out. After checking further into it, I found out that
recidivism was very high, and that nobody was doing
anything about the fact that the institutions are filled*

> up with our people. In 1989, I started the Aboriginal
> Peacekeeeping Unit headquarters, and it was a con-
> stant fight from 1989 to 1995 with management of
> the police department. I was then working solely with
> the Aboriginal community of Toronto and the surround-
> ing area, trying to build bridges and tear down the
> barriers that police had built up over the years. I found
> their attitude towards Aboriginal people very very
> frustrating in that they thought they knew what was
> best for Aboriginal people. In 1995, I retired to open
> Spirit of the People full time to address specifically
> the needs of Aboriginal ex-offenders. We started with
> healing circles once a week and it grew to be very
> successful. We can turn a person around and change
> their lives in a positive cultural and spiritual way. When
> you see that person change it is amazing; you cannot
> buy that.

Bob also expressed some frustration with the lack of interest by governments in funding badly needed programs like those of Spirit of the People. He says some are only beginning now to listen, explaining that the federal government had recently began operation of a program for inmates in the last six months of their sentences to help them reintegrate into society, but it is truly not enough. As Spirit of the People proves itself not to be a "fly-by-night" operation and builds a successful reputation, Bob has hope that this will inspire confidence in establishing more organizations like it.

The key to the success of Spirit of the People, Bob feels, is the emphasis on Native family values, culture, traditions, and language. These are the factors that have been eroded in the lives of so many Aboriginal people through residential schools, foster care, and other forms of attempts to assimilate Native people. The negative effects of these are unfortunately intergenerational and it can take some time to reclaim what has been taken. As far as Bob is concerned, the only solution for Aboriginal people is through self-empowerment. As described in the Spirit of the People literature, the consequences of the oppression faced by Aboriginal people at the systemic level and lived by Aboriginal ex-offenders are clear,

> Upon release, the ex-offender has no place to call home. There is no money for food, shelter or basic necessities, just a bus ticket to the city. There are no advisors, mentors, counsellors, or professionals to turn to who have an understanding of the unique situation faced by Aboriginal ex-offenders. Inadequate interpersonal skills are real barriers to returning to society. The ex-offender is cut off from traditional cultural values and spirituality. Often, the ex-offender has been cut off from society for many years and may find life in a large urban setting baffling and upsetting. With a lack of family or community ties, the ex-offender will often drift back into substance abuse, criminal activity, and eventually, prison (Spirit of the People, 1996).

The greatest difficulties in adjustment are, of course, faced by those who were long-term inmates. Bob related the stories of a couple of ex-offenders to illustrate,

> *There is one guy, who just got out not too long ago, who was doing life. He has been out a month and it is only now that he will step outside his apartment! He is so afraid. The fear of open space. They do not know how to do anything because everything has changed so much. They might as well be on Mars. We have to walk them through everything, as well as try to rebuild their self-esteem. You have to tell them they can do things on their own without somebody telling them to do it. The jailhouse mentality takes such a long*

111

*time to get rid of. A lot of them can't hack it and they
end up going back in because inside you are a 'somebody.' You have the respect of your peers. Out here
you go back to being nothing. You can imagine the
fear and hopelessness that sets in.*

*Getting a job is probably the hardest thing because
they have a huge gap in their resume. Spirit of the
people has plans to start our own construction company so that when they come out, they can work for
this organization without being defeated by their own
resumes. I know a guy who was in for a couple of
years and when he came out he had resumes all over.
But because he could not get a job, he went out and
committed some crime and he's back in jail. I went to
bat for him because I liked him and he is such a big,
gentle person. Everyone feared him because of his size.
I went to court for him and got his sentence reduced.
Getting a job is so important. You can help them spir-
itually, and culturally but if you don't meet all the needs
in that circle, they're going to break apart.*

Spirit of the People is not exclusive to men, and has an ongoing
case-load of women, too. The majority of the Board of Directors are
women, and there are some cultural programs delivered directly to Aboriginal women in the Kingston Prison for Women, including sweats, and a
yearly pow wow. Working in association with the Native Women's Resource Centre, counselling and literacy programs are also being offered at
Spirit of the People. Bob was somewhat distraught regarding the women,
"Their stories are very, very sad, and we have some women doing some
hard, hard time -- they have children, families, ex-husbands, drugs, pros-
titution; I'm telling you, their stories are very sad."

In April of 1997, Bob was recognized for his outstanding work
with Spirit of the People with an Award of Merit from the St. George

Society of Toronto; founded in 1834, it is Toronto's oldest charitable organization. Also this year, in the Native community, Bob was bestowed with the highest possible honour when he was given an Eagle feather at the Traditional Awareness Gathering hosted every year by the Native Canadian Centre. Being orphaned at a young age may have robbed him of his childhood, but it also enabled Bob to discover strength within himself to survive,

> *I went from a little person to an adult, and don't ever remember being a child; but I have a lot of determination and I have visions. I am not a quitter. I see a big change from when I was young to how it is with youth today. I'm so proud of them, they want to know who they are, and they're going to be the leaders of tomorrow. We're going to have many people who are going to know exactly who they are, where they're going, balancing their lives, having their culture together, and it's going to turn around. I see a positive pot of gold at the end of the rainbow.*

Gajic

Aleta-Jo Horsnell

"I am going to be a policeman..."

Aleta-Jo Horsnell is 27 years old, and is Dene, of the Chipewyan First Nation of the North West Territories. Her mother, Alice, is from Fort Resolution, a small community about five hours away from Yellowknife. Aleta-Jo's father, Clyde, is a retired Royal Canadian Mounted Police Officer who was stationed at Fort Smith, NWT when he met and married Aleta-Jo's mother. They had one son, Shawn, and then Clyde joined the Ontario Provincial Police. He was stationed in Northern Ontario, and that is where Aleta-Jo was born. After a few years, Clyde wanted to return to his original home of Nova Scotia, so he rejoined the RCMP and the family lived in a small town there for a number of years. Aleta-Jo grew up and attended high school in Nova Scotia. She competed the Toronto Metro Police Cadet Program in 1988, and became a constable in 1991. She is now a police officer working in the Aboriginal Peacekeeping Unit of the Metropolitan Toronto force.

It was at a very early age that Aleta-Jo realized she would follow in her father's footsteps and become a "policeman." As a child she recalls always repeating to her dad, and anyone else who would listen, "I am going to be a policeman!" Her parents would (and still do occasionally) tease her for saying "policeman" and not "policewoman," but at the time in the early 1970s, women were only beginning to enter police forces, and Aleta-Jo feels that her experience says a lot about how we are socialized to think about gender,

> *I never used to say policewoman. My mom used to always laugh at that. It was kind of ironic because at the time, I think it was 1974, that was when the first female police constable was accepted into the RCMP. Up until then they weren't even considered regular constables. So it was funny even at that age no one ever told me that there was no such thing as a female Mountie. I just assumed that there would be.*

Aleta-Jo also explained that the fact that her family was always very open and honest about her dad's profession, particularly the risks and dangers of it, allowed her from a very early age to appreciate and not fear this line of work. Although her mother did have expectable reservations about her daughter entering police work, Aleta-Jo was encouraged to pursue whatever career of her choice, even if it did seem like something unusual for a young girl to be thinking about. Her mother would always say, "Well, there aren't enough Indian cops in this country," however, she would use the same justification to encourage Aleta-Jo towards other professions too, for that matter, "I thought about being a lawyer, and that was something my mom was big on because she figured lawyers don't get stabbed or have bullets flying at them!" Aleta-Jo toyed with ideas about other professions, too, as a teenager. She considered being a veterinarian since she has always had a great love for animals and nature. But, she was quick to explain that she "couldn't imagine having to put an animal down,"

> *I felt I wouldn't have the guts to do that, but I don't have that problem being a police officer -- I still haven't figured that one out yet. It is also part of the culture. We are taught about nature, and that's the first thing my mother is very big on, and about animals. If anything I've taken that to the extreme, especially when I was younger, I was very much against hunting. As a child I would cry watching 'Bambi' when his mother would get killed. But, my mom explained that if people are eating Bambi's mother to feed their children it's okay, but when people hunt these animals just for their antler racks it's not okay. Growing up, a lot of the people I met would be white people who would hunt just to get the biggest set of racks, which I know is not the best meat because it is older and tough. So, in the past year especially I have made an effort to learn more about animals and traditional ways of hunting, and I have gone hunting.*

Aleta-Jo would always return to the idea of being a police officer, and explained further how both her parents were influential when it came to her deciding on her career. Petite, at 5'3" (5'4" in regulation boots), Aleta-Jo thanks her father for teaching her to have the kind of confidence in herself required to do her job -- that it doesn't matter how big or small an officer is, but what is inside that counts. As she says, it is the way she projects herself that will indicate the way people will respond to her. Again, her mother's influences also come into this, as she explains,

> *To get a person to do what you want, it's the way you communicate to them. If you communicate to a person, 'you are going to do what I tell you to do,' in a certain tone and mannerism, then that person will most likely do what you request of them. If you are unsure of yourself, that person will pick up on that and probably do the opposite. My mother has also taught me that, now that I'm a mother myself [having a four year-old son], that there is this thing called my 'mom voice' and I always recall my mother, at certain times when something was happening that she didn't like -- if she wanted us to 'cease and desist,' she used her 'mom voice'. So both my parents are connected in different ways to my being a police officer.*

As a member of the Aboriginal Peacekeeping Unit, Aleta-Jo and her partner, who is Mig 'maq, have the responsibility of conducting lectures to uniform officers about Aboriginal people, history and culture, based on their own personal knowledge. As Aleta-Jo explained, they need to allow a lot of time for questions during their teaching sessions because of the many misconceptions out there about Aboriginal people. Often, for example, an officer might think it is alright to refer to an Aboriginal woman by the well-known derogatory term reaffirmed by Hollywood stereotypes, and as Aleta-Jo noted, "We have to explain to them that it's not alright and, in fact, it's actually an insult!"

Gajic

Aleta-Jo's mother was a very strong influence on her, instilling in her the cultural and traditional teachings of her people. Aleta-Jo remembers,

> *I was always taught that I was Indian. My mom al-
> ways said that was who she was and consequently,
> that's who I am. I've never heard her call herself Na-
> tive -- only Indian. We travelled quite a bit, when I
> was young, especially in the United States. My mother
> was never the stereotypical Aboriginal woman, with
> braids, so whenever she was asked about her nation-
> ality her reply would be Native-Indian and they would
> understand. We didn't go to church so we were not
> Christians per se, but my mother would talk about
> the Great Spirit and other people. I would notice my-
> self say 'Creator' and she would say that was a south-
> ern term, and where we came from we would say
> 'Great Spirit.'*

> *My mother worked for the Union of Nova Scotia In-
> dians and, growing up in a small town, my contact
> with other Aboriginal people would be at conferences
> or pow wows she took me to. But, on the day-to-day,
> I wasn't brought up on a reserve, and some Aborigi-
> nal people would think that because they grew up on
> a reserve they will be a better Indian than someone
> who didn't. Whereas my mother taught me that is not
> an appropriate thing -- Aboriginal people are distinct
> everywhere in this country. My mother was a Dene
> woman living in Nova Scotia, and there were prob-
> ably not a lot of other Dene women there, but that
> didn't make her any 'less than' the Mig'maq people
> she associated with. The ironic thing is that Fort Reso-
> lution is not even a reserve. In fact, in the North West*

118

Territories, if I'm not mistaken, there is only one reserve and that is the Hay River Reserve. 80% of the NWT population is Aboriginal, so if there was a reserve, it would have to be the whole of the NWT! And so, I look the NWT as being the largest 'reserve' in Canada -- the largest territory of Aboriginal people.

In high school, Aleta-Jo was active in soccer, volleyball, basketball, track and field, and badminton. Sports were very much a social activity for her and she claims that she didn't always concentrate as much on her studies as she should have. She completed her high school and was accepted into the Toronto Metro Police Cadets Program, even before graduation. Sometimes, in hindsight, she feels that it might have been even more beneficial to have carried on with her academic career with a college or university degree. She, does not, however, rule out the possibility of taking this direction in the future, explaining that there are good opportunities for promotions and advancement in the police force when one has a degree of higher education.

Aleta-Jo greatly emphasizes how important her sense of family is, a trait she inherited from both her mother's and her father's different cultures. Her father, who is of English background, taught her that she should never put her family in a position that they should feel they need to ask for help, explaining that, "it is just a given that you will help your family." Aleta-Jo's brother, Shawn, currently lives in the United States where he has a wife and daughter. She and her brother are very close even though they don't see or talk to one another on a regular basis. Each is comfortable knowing that they do not have to hear from each other all the time to know that they care deeply about one another. It is simply a basic understanding of sharing, caring, and respect. She remembers one incident from her high school years which left a lasting impression on her,

I was going to a party with my girlfriends, and it was also the first time I tried alcohol. When I came home my parents were aware that I had been drinking, and

they told me that they would figure out my punishment the next day. When I got up the next day, I wasn't feeling very well and that was almost justice enough! But, my parents decided that my punishment would be not playing sports for one month, and this was at a very critical period. The provincial finals for track and field were scheduled during my punishment time, and I had been ranked third in the province, and it was also during the same time as my soccer team's final matches. As a result, the next year I was a little bit behind the rest of the competitors. Instead of being ranked third, I was relegated to sixth place. I don't begrudge them for teaching me that lesson. It still gives me shivers, just thinking about it, because it was a tough pill to swallow. The whole experience taught me something very important. If someone takes something meaningful and worthwhile away from you, because you acted inappropriately, it really makes you think.

Another very important person in Aleta Jo's life, of course, is her young son Chip, who at age four, also aspires to be a police officer. Aleta Jo added that she did not name him Chip after the TV show, *My Three Sons*, but that Chip is short for Chipewyan, the name of his grandmother's people. Aleta-Jo doesn't shelter Chip from the realities of her job. She teaches him that the main reason there are police are to keep everyone safe.

She doesn't think it is appropriate for any parent to shelter their child from a realistic, tangible problem or situation. She feels that, by not telling children the truth you teach them to lie, and suggests that might be why there are some of the problems that exist today, not only in the Aboriginal community, but in society in general. When asked if her son understands her position as a police officer, Aleta-Jo replied,

*He knows I'm a police officer; he even calls me a 'po-
liceman' sometimes, so I have to correct him! I think
it's important that he realize that there are police-
women and that there is a difference between men
and women. His father is also a police officer so he
gets it from both of us. He is also aware that his grandfather was with the RCMP. Sometimes, on our way to
daycare, he'll say that he doesn't want to go, but wants
to go to work with me. I have to explain to him that I
have to do police work and he protests, "I'm a policeman; I'm a policeman!" and I say, "Maybe someday
you will be, when you grow up."*

Between being an officer of the law and a mother, Aleta-Jo finds
time to volunteer with several organizations in the Aboriginal community.
She is a past President of the Board of Directors of Anduhyaun Inc. which
provides a shelter for women, second-stage housing for Native single
mothers and their families, and a daycare. She has also served terms on
the Board of Directors for Pedahbun Lodge, a substance-abuse treatment agency. All her volunteer work is done on her own time, apart from
her duties with the police services. And yet, Aleta-Jo still manages to find
time for herself. She's an avid reader, saying she just about "catches cabin
fever" if she doesn't have something to read. Her literary menu includes
anything from Popular Mechanics to National Geographic to crime novels.
She looks at reading as an investment, referring to it as "brain exercise."
She has recently started jogging and hopes to start playing on a women's
soccer team. Her real incentive to get physically moving again was her
son, Chip. She feels it is important to stimulate both his brain and his body.
Aleta-Jo's philosophy for life today relies heavily on what her mother taught
her. She used to tell her to be careful about the way she behaved because,
"what you do to others may come back and hit you in the backside some
day!" She is a believer in not continuing a cycle of wrong-doing, concluding,
"People should behave honourably even if they don't particularly like the
other person or agree with what they are saying -- it is the teaching of the
circle."

121

Gajic

Harvey Manning

"We do have little paths that we get people started on..."

Harvey Manning is of the Eagle Clan, and is from the Stoney Point First Nation (Ojibway) near Sarnia, Ontario. Born in 1960, Harvey comes from a large family of eleven children. As Harvey explained with a laugh, Toronto has been an on-and-off home for him for the last 21 years; in a way, trouble brought him to the city, and helping others with their own troubles has been a large factor in what has kept Harvey in Toronto,

> *I was forced to come to Toronto. When I was fifteen I got in trouble back home so they told me to leave town or I was going to face charges. My mother sent me to a Christian boys home up here on Broadview Ave. and ever since then I have been in and out of Toronto. I've tried to move away many times - to Phoenix, Vancouver, Winnipeg, and I've always come back. It's mostly the people. I have been here so long. All my friends are here. Right now it is Anishnawbe Health Centre that draws me here because they have got so many traditional people and programs. I am just growing quickly, learning about my traditions.*

Ten years ago, when the Native Centre was celebrating its 25th anniversary, Harvey was working there on maintenance. For the last five years, Harvey has been working off-and-on with the Anishnawbe Health Street Patrol van, which scouts Toronto's streets keeping a look out for people living on the streets who may need a sandwich, some warm clothes, a sleeping bag, medical attention, or just someone to talk to. Harvey has really found his niche in this work, as he talks about it from personal experience, and with great understanding and compassion,

Gajic

In the late 1980s, there was a guy named Clarence Southwind and he lived on the streets where he had a lot of friends. He quit drinking, but still spent a lot of time with the guys out there just talking with them and seeing how they were doing. He thought about taking out food and sandwiches, and he started by carrying stuff in a knapsack. It got bigger and bigger so people started to drive him in vans, and that is how Street Patrol got started.

I started out as a volunteer working with George McCloud with Street Patrol. I find all different ages on the street from youth to older people. I have seen myself in a lot of these people. I spent a lot of time living at the Salvation Army and Seaton House, not having a place to go or a place to eat. I remember when I was quite a bit younger, I was all over the city and I was drinking a lot. I have seen many of those things about me on the streets, so it just made my job easier to do. I could relate, I was really happy to do it. I know where a lot of the guys are coming from. Street Patrol is a kind of first-hand contact with the people on the streets. We try to bring them into Anishnawbe Health and from there, if they want help, we try to get them off the street, into housing or treatment centres.

An innovative initiative that Harvey has been involved in for the past few years, is a summer camping program. This program highlights how stressful it is on a person to live on the streets worrying about potential violence, illness, and whether it will be possible to eat and sleep every day. Getting a few people out of the city to go camping gives them a chance to have a "vacation" from all of that, as well as a very much-needed opportunity to simply reflect on their lives, and benefit from some traditional teachings as well,

124

We have a camping program where I take the guys camping every summer. There are about eight or nine people and we'll go once or twice in the summer. Sometimes it works out funny — I try to have a certain list of guys but I know it never, ever works out. Like last year, we went driving down the alleys looking for guys and we found 'Beak' passed out. So we just stopped the van and threw him in and we took him with us. We camp down at Stony Point. It is really isolated with a big private beach and you just see a different kind of person when you take them out there. Their defenses are right down. We just hang out and oftentimes we'll sit around the fire, tell stories and talk about our lives.

At first we used to bring guys with us to do sweats and we are going to do that again this year. We try to bring people to come and talk about traditions. We've taken quite a few women in the past, too. We had a woman come down and do sweats for the women. It was great, they loved it. It really makes people think about their lives. It gives them that chance to just be alone and think about what they want to do and I think it helps them a lot. Everybody talks about it all winter long. I have got a couple of guys who want to start organizing it. That is really good for them to help organize things and get it ready. They can't wait to get out there! It gives them an incentive.

As successful as the camping trips are, however, Harvey feels that they will not ultimately lead to anyone getting off the streets as a result. "Two weeks is not going to compare to years and years of abuse on the streets," he explains. Harvey related this to a similar problem with treatment centres, where government regulations limit a person's stay to only 28

125

days in most cases. Many different people require a variety of means to deal with not only addiction problems, but psychological, social, and spiritual issues as well, and for many, the 28-day limitation creates barriers for their recovery. Harvey felt that, given the time, a good number of people coming through Anishnawbe Health do have a chance to get control of their addictions, as he further illustrated,

> *We see it all the time. We try to give them a path to follow. There is one young guy who has been coming here for about a year now but he would never really talk. He would just come and do his laundry or have a coffee, and kind of show up two or three times a week. Finally, he says to me, 'You know, I'd like to get involved,' and I said, 'It is about time!' I told him about the camping, I told him about drumming, and he said he used to sing. I told him about the sweats that we go to, and he is getting involved. We do have little paths that we get people started on. We see how they progress and then we try to get them into treatment centres eventually. If they fall off their path, you never discourage them, you encourage them to come back. Everyone falls off; you just keep on trying.*

Like many people who work on the front lines of the social needs in the Native community, Harvey emphasized a connection between alcohol and drug abuse, and Native people's history with residential schools, foster care, and, in many cases, "adoption-out" (into non-Native families),

> *I've asked a lot of the guys about their backgrounds, and probably the majority of the Native people on the streets have either been adopted out or have been to residential schools. I think that tells you a lot right there — just being taken away from your family. When you take children away and put them in the residential*

school that is tearing the family apart and, of course,
it is going to be hard for the parents not to drink. And
who do you blame? I do not blame those parents for
starting to drink after their children were stolen by
these churches, organizations and governments — they
are to blame and that is the bottom line.

In addition, Harvey only sees the needs of street people getting greater, "Just in the last couple of years I have seen it almost double; I see a lot more people on the street, a lot more youth, a lot more Native people." This last summer, Harvey, along with many other representatives of organizations who work with the homeless in Toronto, have noticed a huge jump in numbers. With unemployment at an all-time high, particularly in the Native community, and as the ultra-conservative provincial government implement their agenda including changes to the Landlord and Tenant's Act, for example, many more people are forced out.

While Harvey stressed that funding is a constant problem for Street Patrol to keep going and to meet the rising demands of increased numbers of people living on the streets of Toronto, he also explained that there is no shortage of good will. Many, many volunteers help out every night the van goes out — rain, shine, or in sub-sub-zero temperatures. Volunteers need to sign up in advance, and they undergo a small screening process to ensure they are suitable for the job. The Patrol is usually booked up to a month and a half ahead all the time because there are so many who want to help. Many are very dedicated, and return often, or work regularly.

Harvey emphasized that the participation of Native volunteers was particularly significant in that it is an all-around excellent learning experience for them. They get to interact with the people who have been the most marginalized and stereotyped among Native people, and it opens their eyes to some of their own misconceptions about street people, as well as about themselves. Harvey would really like to see more young Native people volunteer with Street Patrol, as it is in his words, "a real education."

One of the key issues that many have difficulty understanding is why people stay on the streets for many years, even though they may have alternatives, such as in some cases, the possibility to return to their First Nations home communities. Harvey explained that while for some Native people, "going home" is an option, most find a sense of belonging and strong community with other people living on the streets,

> *A lot of their friends are right here on the street and it is a very close community. Everybody knows each other and they look after each other and they are fairly happy. I think a lot of them want to get off the street. I know guys that have been on the street for over twenty years and something finally hits them and they say, 'Hey it's time for me to move on,' and they do get off the streets. After that many years on the street — their bodies — they can't cope with working after that. They have a hard time fitting back into the mainstream, and I don't see a lot of the guys who get off the street out at the community gatherings or anything.*

In discussing deaths on the streets, Harvey was candid in his opinion, particularly in relation to media treatment of the subject,

> *I don't think deaths can be stopped on the streets. It is always going to happen. Even when the police talk about putting in these new laws to pull people off the streets, that's not going to help, that is not going to stop it either. I believe that Street Patrol prevents deaths but that is something you do not hear about in the newspapers or the media. The media likes to build on tragedies — things that people will feel. I believe that Street Patrol prevents deaths, I know it does. The 'Open Hotline' for street people worked out pretty well. I got a lot of response. If it was freezing you phoned a hotline and they would get hold of Street Patrol or Roaming Patrol and we would try to find a place for*

these guys to sleep if it was too cold out. If someone just looked at how someone got on the street or had an open mind and thought about things, especially about Native people, it would not be long before they come up with a clear answer and they would probably understand. But there are so many narrow-minded people in this country they do not think about how so many people end up on the streets.

Finally, Harvey refers to his personal experience to reiterate the importance of Native culture, not just for self-discovery, but to contribute to building a strong and healthy Native community. The process can be a long one filled as much with the un-learning of negatives in many Native lives, as with the continued learning of the positives of Native culture,

It took me a long time to get back. To come this way. I went to a treatment centre probably about seven or eight ago and ever since then I have been searching. I have been going to sweats, going to fasts, and it is not easy. It is hard to get the things you have been taught all your life about how bad Indian people are and how dirty Indian people are. That is what you grew up with and it really made you ashamed. I am not that way anymore or else I would not be here. I would probably be still drunk some place. I am very proud of who I am and the things I do. It has taken a long time for me to get that out of my mind, and get that Christianity stuff out of my mind. I had that forced on me for so many years. I had a hard time trying to figure out traditions and Christianity and separate the two. Finally, I have done that. Ten years ago, I was sitting on the same bar stool I had been on for years and years. In the last five years I have accomplished a lot. I feel really good about myself, the things I have done and the people I work with.

Gajic

Frances Sanderson

"Some say shyness is a characteristic of Native people... I say it's intimidation."

Energy, determination, and a very good heart, are the words one immediately thinks of to describe Frances Sanderson. Although Frances has worked directly in the Native community in Toronto for only three years as the Executive Director of Nishnawbe Homes Inc., a non-profit housing organization, she has brought with her an incredible wealth of experience in terms of both her business knowledge, and her sense of Aboriginal culture.

Frances was born in Toronto in the late 1940s, and grew up in the East York area. Her father was of Spanish origin, and her mother was one of ten children born to Victoria and Augustine McGregor, a prominent family of the Ojibway Whitefish First Nation (Birch Island) on the northeastern part of Lake Huron. Like many young Native women in the late 1930s, Frances' mother, Colleen came to Toronto for work and an education. After careful consideration by her parents, Colleen and her sister Lillian set off for Toronto; Lillian had a career in nursing, while Colleen married and became a stay-at-home mother to six children.

When Frances was a teenager, she recalls that the family could not afford "the finer things that all teenage girls want," so her mother suggested Frances find a job. At the age of 15, Frances started working in the snack bar of the local bowling centre, a move that would determine a great deal of the rest of her life. Frances was quite happy with this job since it was in a recreational place and had a happy atmosphere. And, given she had already been preparing meals for a family of eight for ten years, she said, "I had been helping my mother in the kitchen, lifting burgers, making soup, hot dogs, and toast for years feeding my younger sisters; that was something I knew how to do." Frances was pleased to be paid 75 cents an hour for something she had been doing all this time for free. She paid some rent, but was able to buy her own stockings, make-up, and get her hair done (which she wore in the beehive style). She really enjoyed her teenagehood, listening to Elvis, talking about the Beatles and socializing. In retrospect, Frances reflected on the differences that being Native meant to her, and to later generations of teenagers,

> *From the time I was young, I was always proud to be an Indian, as that was what they called us then. People were fascinated by it because nobody knew any Indians. They thought there weren't any around. They were around but were passed by so often. When I did tell people I was Indian I was treated special. I didn't have the negativism that a lot of other Native people have had. I was proud to be who I was. I went to school in the public system, not the Catholic system, so there was a lot more ethnicity, and so there were many other cultures as well. In the fifties and early sixties we just talked about make up and hair. We were not as politically involved as kids are now. We were far more naive about things. It didn't come directly in the front door of our house either. My parents were not politically active, they just tried to do the best they could.*

Frances' determination was certainly evident from an early age, she says that at the age of 12 she already knew what she would do with her life — get married, have children, and a successful career in the work force. At 17, Frances met her husband at the bowling centre, and they have been married for 30 years. They have two married daughters, and two grandsons who are their pride and joy. And, Frances did not sit idly watching others enjoying the game of bowling from behind her snack bar counter, she began to play, and given the drive she has, she went on to be a Canadian and international champion at the game. She was captain of the Canadian Women's Team which bowled all over the world, and missed going to the Olympics in Seoul, Korea by being only ten pins out of first place. Although that was a disappointment for her, Frances was rated in the top five in Canada for 15 years, was inducted into the Greater Toronto Hall of Fame, and the Provincial Hall of Fame. At the present time, she still holds bowling records in North America, South America and Central America, saying somewhat understately, "When I take on something that I believe in, and have a passion for it, I will reach my goal."

Frances continued to work for the bowling centre for 30 years, and it grew into a significant company over the years, opening and running 30 other bowling centres. As the company expanded, Frances rose in the ranks along with it. When she left three years ago, she was Vice-President of Promotion, Publicity and Advertisement. Near the end of her employment with the bowling company she felt she was beginning to become stagnant, and that her job was not providing the same challenge as it once had. Meanwhile, she had taken on a number of responsibilities with a number of charity organizations she volunteered with such as the Variety Club of Ontario, and the Greater Toronto Women's Bowling Association, the White Ribbon campaign, and the Softball Association.

She had also began to get much more involved in the Aboriginal community, first sitting on the Board of Directors of Nishnawbe Homes, and of the Native Canadian Centre, as well as attending community functions and activities at the Native Canadian Centre. Frances states her philosophy simply, "If you can't be a part of the solution then you are part of the problem; I wasn't one to offer criticism without taking part in it as well, so that's what I did."

When the job of Executive Director at Nishnawbe Homes came up, she jumped at it. "It was an opportunity to do something for my own people, and to do something that was rewarding, and challenging." Even though Frances had no experience being employed in the non-profit business, or with tenants, she had confidence that her strong administrative background would serve her well. In her three years as Executive Director, she has seen the finalization of construction for their first apartment building, the Maddy Harper Lodge on Jones Avenue, and they have a 100% occupancy, however, this has created new frustrations in that now, Nishnawbe Homes has too many applicants and not enough units. Frances explains how a careful balance of her experience has helped her do her job, "Because I was raised in the corporate white world, with years in non-Native business, I picked up a lot of ways, and I try to bring them to my life now; I try to blend the two cultures together as best I can. Networking, one of Frances' stronger suits, helps a lot with this issue,

> *I haven't burned any of my bridges. I will turn to my friends in the bowling business and say we need something, or organize the bowl-a-thon for the Centre for example. Or I might talk to someone at the Variety Club for advice. I often call on them all for assistance. There are a lot of good people who will help out if they are asked in the right way. You have to take the proper route. It is like with our Elders, there is a way to approach them for something, the offering of tobacco and recognizing the fact they are respected and are thought highly of in the community. I think the same thing goes for anyone you are dealing with. You need to respect and not expect it.*

Frances also indicates that without networking in the community, a lot of people would go without being looked after. She very much acknowledges the work of organizations like Na-Me-Res, Council Fire, Anishnawbe Health, and Street Patrol who help the many who can't get into the very limited subsidized housing. Frances knows that these organizations are always seeing increases in their workloads, and she sees only growing numbers on her waiting lists. She is very fearful of what will happen to Aboriginal people especially with the current threats to subsidized housing. She explains how their situation differs from that in the general population,

> *Many Aboriginal people are on general welfare assistance, family benefits, or unemployment benefits. Many are being funded from their bands for education and are going to school. They have grants and*

scholarships but they don't have a job. If I was in the business of only housing people with jobs I wouldn't be dealing with only Aboriginal people. I would be dealing with the people who could afford to pay me. If we lose non-profit Aboriginal housing, where are our people going to go? We are absolutely in the throws of possibly losing what we have. The federal government is wanting to download to the provincial government. The provincial government doesn't want to be in the housing business, so they will download to municipalities. The municipalities cannot afford the subsidies that are involved to look after these things. They are going to go to the private sector. They're going to go to market rent and the people that are in a low income level will not be able to afford it.

Frances suggests that there is a great need for even more networking in the Aboriginal community. She sees each of the almost 50 distinct Aboriginal service agencies in Toronto as a spoke in one big wheel. She spoke of the Native Canadian Centre as a vital spoke in this wheel particularly in its capacity as a meeting place for people, and because it is often the first place Aboriginal people, new to the city, will come,

There really is a strong network of Friendship Centres throughout Ontario and across Canada. They have Friendship Centres in every big city. It's sort of like the Aboriginal YMCA. It's a gathering place for them. Though I am urbanized as much as anybody else, I went to look for the Friendship Centre when I was in Vancouver. It was a connection; it was a nice brown face on the other side of the conversation that you are comfortable with. They know when they are coming to Toronto, so arrangements can be made in advance. Not all people are as sophisticated as

> *Torontonians. A lot come from small towns or villages
> outside of Toronto. It is pretty imposing when you first
> get here, especially if you don't know anyone. When
> the need has arisen, the Native Centre has helped many
> people with health care, translation and
> accommodations.*

Frances added, there is also a need for an Aboriginal political entity in Toronto to serve the best interests of the community as a whole without the restrictions or special interests of being run by one of the non-profit agencies themselves, "a form of umbrella organization that we would all sit under and be protected by." Frances uses the analogy of the band councils on reserves where the system is at least supposed to work to offer some representation and governance,

> *... and some reserves have only 200 or 300 people
> and there are more than 65,000 Native people here in
> Toronto; the Native people are sitting in a great big
> boat with no oars, just floating around in the corporate
> white world — we have no captain, no compass, and
> no power— we have no control over our destiny when
> we have no one in the seat of authority and there is no
> one to speak for urban Aboriginal people. The chiefs
> and council on reserves have funding and they have
> direct ties with the government which has a strong
> hold on Native affairs. Because we are urban and
> because the government doesn't recognize us as
> needing as much, or any assistance, they are pretty
> much turning their back on urban Aboriginal people.
> If the kind of leadership we need should ever come to
> be, we would become a force to be reckoned with —
> as a sitting group of 65,000 voters, don't you think
> the politicians in Toronto would listen to us?*

Having not been raised in an Aboriginal community, Frances is now beginning to really learn what that sense of community is about, understanding what she refers to when she says we are "communal" as a people, "We look after our own which is why you don't see a great many Aboriginal nursing homes and Aboriginal people in long-term facilities with nobody coming to visit. We have to, as a group, make the effort to look after these people." Presenting a willingness to learn is the first step towards gaining an understanding and pride in Aboriginal identity,

There are people who want to teach you. I'm willing to do anything to educate myself about my ancestors, the history of my culture and of my spirituality. I love to listen, and I love the art and what it means. It seems that I can learn so much from my Elders on the reserve and in the community. For the Elders they have knowledge in their stories when talking to you, because they talk honestly. They do not use fifty-dollar words, they use ten cent words. They are speaking from their hearts and I love that. More and more, young people are using Elders for what they are supposed to be used for. That is what is so particular about our culture and our traditions. We revere our Elders and we respect our Elders. We don't put them off into nursing homes and never see them again. We use them. Some would say we use them possibly to death! Some of the Elders are used until death because our Elders have a wealth of knowledge and they teach right to the very end; how they approach things, how they see things. I see an Elder differently now, than I did 30 years ago. I see things a lot differently. Those who are 30 years older than me see things a lot differently as well. I do see the kids going to the Elders. They are making sure there is an Elder on a Committee, making sure there is an Elder present when they are

137

> *doing things, and making sure they approach the*
> *Elders properly. This is coming from the urbanized*
> *Aboriginal people; children born here and raised here.*

Frances is also very adamant about the vitality of a good strong formal education, emphasizing how opportunities for Aboriginal people now are much greater than they were when she was younger. It was difficult, she points out, for an Aboriginal person to maintain their identity and get an education; the two were seen as incompatible, "Now, I see more and more people knowing the way to fight fire is with fire — they are going to work corporately and getting a job corporately and fighting them on their own terms." Having done well in school and in the corporate world herself, Frances thanks her mother especially as a model for her determination and inspires young people to do the same,

> *My mother was very determined. Not only was she*
> *determined to make a life for herself and her family,*
> *she was determined for us to get a good education. I*
> *have a drive that pushes me to do the best I can all*
> *the time; that is what I did. I would have been*
> *successful had I been on a reserve, too, I think. I would*
> *have started a business, even if it was taking in*
> *laundry, having a small store or doing income tax. I*
> *would have found something for me to do. I am not*
> *good at sitting doing nothing. The only sure thing I*
> *know is to go to work and work hard at a job. I am a*
> *workaholic - ask anyone who knows me. I enjoy*
> *coming to work, and I come in at 7:30 a.m. I have*
> *the work done before business hours at 9:00 a.m., and*
> *then I can have time to counsel tenants. I help them*
> *with financial counseling. Many are struggling and*
> *can't make ends meet because they are on welfare and*
> *they don't know how they are going to pay their bills,*
> *and they fall behind in their rent. But we have a*

mortgage on these places, so if I help them, it helps out all around for them to get a handle on their financial difficulties. I see myself as a softer, gentler landlord — a landlord with a heart is something you don't run into very much out there.

Some say shyness is a common characteristic to a lot of Native people and we don't know exactly where it came from, but it's been there all our lives. I think it's intimidation, to be treated as a second-class citizen, made to feel like 10 cents worth of dirty soap. That is what we had to fight back. I never had that problem. I am not intimidated by large crowds. I'll get nervous, but I will still stand up and speak. I am not afraid of it. I have as much right as anyone else. I have a right to speak my mind and say what I think. I've always been sort of full of myself: saw myself as special. I have a reason to be here, as much right, as anyone else sitting where I am sitting.

Gajic

Ramona Toulouse
"My whole life has filled up so much"

The greatest hope for the future of Native communities across the country rests in the fact that youth account for the largest segment of the population, reaching up to 55% in some communities. The Toronto Native community is no different; approximately 50% of the total Native population in the city is under the age of 24. Therefore, as the future leaders of the community, a great emphasis is placed on the importance of nurturing families and young people, listening attentively to their concerns and needs, and educating them in traditional ways. Ramona Toulouse's experience and vision reverberates strongly with this perspective.

Ramona is Ojibway, and was born at Sagamok First Nation which is about an hour's drive west of Sudbury, Ontario. At the age of 20, she is a single mom to a beautiful toddler, Amethyst, and she has volunteered extensively in the Native community in Toronto, putting her efforts especially into activities involving youth. She spent most of her life in Hamilton, but returned to live at Sagamok when she was 13 where she stayed for about three years with her Auntie. Finding life on the reserve too stifling, at 16 she set off on her own to live in Sudbury. At about the same time Ramona was settling into Sudbury, her mother moved to Toronto, and Ramona decided to visit her mom over the Christmas holidays, expecting to go home early in the New Year. But, once she was introduced into the Toronto Native community, she decided to stay,

The culture was everywhere and they were proud of it. Before then, I always felt like I was the only Indian person around, I was just a person with a status card. At first, I was afraid of saying something wrong or that I might do something wrong. There are so many things you should know and respect. I was scared I might disrespect and everyone would look at me. It was hard, even now. At first it was out of curiosity because I didn't really know anything about it, but now after

141

> *hearing different people speak and what they say*
> *really makes sense, I want to be proud of it; I want to*
> *keep it going. The birth of my daughter has really put*
> *everything together for me. I want her to grow up to*
> *be proud of herself.*

Ramona related that she had been in trouble at lot when she was younger and had a hard time staying in school. After dropping out of school in grade eleven, Ramona says that she found it difficult to figure out what she wanted to do. She was very mature for her age; most of her friends were five or six years older than her when she was a young teenager. She ended up drinking and smoking, and going to parties because she wanted to fit in with the older crowd and be just like them. She tried hard to fit into their circle, maybe a little too hard. She feels that she left her childhood behind too soon.

Slowly, she became involved and started to put her energy into the Native community, even though she felt that she didn't know much about it. She went places, listening and observing intently. A turning point for her was when she tagged along with her mother who was volunteering at the Native Canadian Centre's annual Traditional Awareness Gathering when she was about 17,

> *I followed my mother around everywhere because I*
> *didn't know anyone. I got the opportunity to sit in on*
> *one of the workshops and heard the Creation story*
> *and thought, 'Wow, a lot of the teachings are so true.'*
> *I had never realized that before. It was like the alarm*
> *for a wake-up call. After that I became really gung-ho*
> *to help out. I wanted to do so much. I was here and*
> *there, and I began to overload myself. I was*
> *volunteering at the Native Centre a lot, and I got a job*
> *placement there working with membership. I got*
> *involved with helping with First Nations Day; that*
> *was a major event. I met a lot of people doing that kind*
> *of stuff. My whole life has filled up so much.*

Determined to do well, Ramona is definite about the path she must take, and says "because I'm young, there are always people who doubt my ability." She finds that young people seem to have to prove themselves every time they take on a new task. "It is difficult," she says because she knows she can do it, and even though she has proven herself to be very thorough and competent, people may still often question her abilities, but she continues, "When all is said and done, it's really a good feeling when everything turns out right. I can say, 'I did it!'"

Not long after she first became involved in the community, she met some other young women who were involved in Native fashion designing, and ended up having the opportunity to do some modelling. She says she was really nervous at first because she did not think she looked like a super model. On her first outing, her knees were shaking so badly, she thought everyone could see them knocking together. After a while she got used to the tension and stress and she started to like the feeling, the rush and the excitement. She soon became very competent and modelled in fashion shows at the Park Plaza Hotel, a smaller show at the Six Nations annual pow wow on the reserve, and at the huge gathering held every year at SkyDome, the Toronto professional sports stadium. On that occasion she will never forget what it was like to see herself on the 'Jumbotron!'

Although she was accepted by a modelling agency she decided to give up this career after the SkyDome show because the agency demanded that she lose a significant amount of weight, she explained, "They said I was too fat -- I am five feet, nine inches tall, and weighed 130 pounds -- they wanted me to lose twenty pounds, and I said forget it. For a while I had envisioned myself as becoming the first Native super-model, but I had a hard time losing that weight, and in the end it was only a passing thing." Reflecting back, Ramona added that she felt she may have never carried on her path of self-discovery, and would have forgotten entirely who she was if she would have carried on with the modelling.

Ramona has remained very active in the community -- she is the youth representative on the Native Canadian Centre's Board of Directors, she also volunteers with the Birds of a Feather -- and alcoholics-anonymous group that uses traditional Native healing techniques, as well as with other agencies in the city. She currently works part time as a librarian at First Nations House at the University of Toronto, and worked for a while prior to that full time with Spirit of the People, an organization to help Native ex-offenders get back on their feet.

At Spirit of the People, Ramona was charged with organizing a traditional youth gathering for Native people aged 13 to 24 to share concerns of youth in the community and how they could relate them to traditional ways. She had to be very creative given it was to be a three-day event and everything needed to be free, since a lot of the youth taking part do not have money. Ramona has fond memories of what turned out to be a very successful event. The 12-person organizing committee she worked with was a great group, and many of them had really good points-of-view, some which took her totally off guard. For example, they wanted to emphasize that the event would be a *Youth*, and not an Elders' gathering, and this led them in quite a different direction than she had expected. They decided the conference topics would deal with issues specific to today's youth, and try to reach out to as large as possible a spectrum of participants ranging from street kids, to young mothers, to youth alcoholics, and ex-offenders. Together, they decided how they would integrate the traditional teachers and Elders they would invite.

Ramona was particularly concerned that they carefully consider how they balance the opportunities for youth to express themselves, with the teachings of the Elders. The gathering attracted about 100 young people and they all enjoyed it immensely. Ramona had been very anxious before the event, but in the end she was happy it went beyond her expectations. Now, as Board member at the Native Centre, she is turning her ideas to interesting youth in community participation on an even greater scale,

> *A lot of young people are afraid to speak out. They're afraid their idea might not be good, or they will be pushed to the side. We feel others decide what we are going to do. We need to listen to youth more, and get them involved. It seems to me people come to the city, and they end up either in the party crowd, or they really*

get into the culture. They may start out partying and realize that's not where they want to be and they go out to the Native Centre, and get involved. So, whether you like it or not, we need to look at the youth more and get them involved. The Centre is a meeting place, and it's the first place people go.

It would be nice if they had somebody there to talk to without having to make an appointment, and were really set up to receive the youth. We have a whole building of seniors next door. We could have some sort of program that got them involved with the youth. It's all in the presentation, you have to get them excited. We need to make them feel comfortable and be acutely aware of their feelings. We don't want them coming and feeling like they will be judged. They have to know it is alright to make a mistake and that they can change. If a person goes out and does something wrong many times and you ignore them, and say there is no hope for them, they are going to keep going out there and they will keep making the same mistakes. You must give them hope that they can do something better for themselves. When you have people who have made mistakes and turned their lives around for the better, you have examples to go by. You can use those examples and show that other people have turned their lives around, so can you.

Ramona believes that one of the reasons young Native people come to the city is to get away from abusive families. She feels that when people are so used to a situation, they may not know that they can behave differently, and have a different life. When they get to the city, they have an opportunity to meet people who will steer them on the right path. Ramona related her experience as an example,

Gajic

> *When I started volunteering I met different people.*
> *There are Executive Directors of the Native*
> *organizations who are friends of mine, and who are*
> *trying to help the community, not only themselves. I*
> *kind of look to them for guidance. I see women, a lot*
> *of women, who are Executive Directors here in*
> *Toronto. I want to be like them. I don't want to stay at*
> *home and not contribute.*

Finally, becoming a young single parent has shaped Ramona's perspective on life considerably causing her to reflect with care on her future and that of her daughter's. Motherhood has changed Ramona's way of thinking. She used to go here and there, visit friends and stay over with them for a while. Now that she has a small child, she's trying to give her daughter a home. She wants her to be comfortable where she is. Ramona feels that her daughter has made her more stable, though she's still adjusting to staying in one spot. Reiterating her concern that Amethyst grow up proud of being an Aboriginal person, she is glad that her mother who helps out considerably with her care speaks to her in Ojibway, and Ramona brings Amethyst around the Native Centre several times each week.

> *There are a lot of young mothers out there. I can't*
> *speak for everybody, but from what I see, there seems*
> *to be a lot of young girls having babies. It's really hard*
> *with a child. I always had this idea in my mind, since*
> *I was a little girl, about being married and having*
> *children. Then I got pregnant and what was I going to*
> *do? Would I be able to take care of a baby? I had a*
> *hard time during my pregnancy. There were a lot of*
> *complications. That experience was really trying, but*
> *now that she's here, I'm adjusting to being a parent.*
> *I would like her to be the complete opposite of myself.*
> *I don't want her to have to go through the things I did.*
> *I want to lay out her path better than mine. It's*

*phenomenal being a mother. It's like nothing I've ever
felt before. I sometimes look at her and all of a sudden,
she's four inches bigger and 20 pounds heavier. I look
at her all the time and she grows so fast. I want for her
everything I never had. I want to teach her the cultural
ways right from birth.*

As far as the future is concerned, Ramona has no definite plans but she does
plan to stay in Toronto. She envisions herself working in the community,
feeling she can accomplish a lot, and make some really valuable
contribution, whether it be in building up a new organization, or helping an
existing one progress to a different level. In the end, everything comes back
to her daughter. Ramona wants her daughter to be proud of her mother and
able to say, "Hey, that's my mom."

Andrew McConnell

"To know where you are going, you have to know where you've been"

Andrew McConnell is a young man in his early 30s, originally from Wausausking First Nation (Parry Island), Ontario. Following a successful football career with the *Edmonton Eskimos*, he is now a Vice-President with the Toronto Dominion Bank. He is strong in his beliefs as an Aboriginal person, as well as being a philosophical thinker by today's standards. As Andrew says, he refers to and lives by his undying respect for Aboriginal traditions and cultural values instilled in him particularly by his grandfather,

> *My grandfather used to always tell me that to know where you're going, you have to know where you've been. And I was fortunate that he spent a lot of time with me as a boy, teaching me to be proud of where I came from, my culture and heritage, my spirituality. I think that to some extent, it gave me a bit of inner strength and allowed me to realize that the only obstacles and barriers that were in place were the ones that I accepted as obstacles and barriers. He told me that education was going to be a key for me to truly make a difference, not only in my own life, but hopefully in trying to walk a good life, in living a good way, in educating myself, and hopefully, in passing that along to other Aboriginal people.*

When he was 15 years old, Andrew came to Toronto where he finished high school. He then went on to St. Francis Xavier University in Nova Scotia and received his degree in Economics. Sports have always been an important part of Andrew's life, and he feels they provided him with an important building block in the foundation on which he has built his success. Whether competitive, recreational or for personal achievement,

Andrew feels all sports are an incredible teacher for young men and women. As he says, "They teach discipline, commitment, team-work, how to win, and most importantly, how to lose gracefully. A lot of what we do in life doesn't reach our expectations and we are not as successful as we would like to be." Consequently, Andrew has been involved in various sports since he was very young, whether it was fishing, running or swimming. In high school he began playing football, and this turned into the opportunity for him to get a post-secondary education. Andrew said that when he started playing football he was relatively a novice. He had thrown a ball a few times, but never really thought of himself as a football player. He had little understanding of the game and soon realized that football can be a fairly complicated game. He persevered, excelled, and ended up being drafted into professional football. By the time he had finished his studies at St. Francis Xavier, he had been selected All-Canadian three times, and the Canadian Football League (CFL) drafted him in the first round, in 1986.

To top things off, Andrew was also drafted by the National Football League (NFL) Cincinnati Bengals. His decision to take on the NFL was one filled with anxiety and excitement, and Andrew faced the challenge head-on. Culture-shock was an understatement for Andrew as he travelled from Parry Island to Toronto, Toronto to Nova Scotia, and finally from Nova Scotia to Cincinnati. Life was certainly becoming an adventure and Andrew says he felt like an explorer seeing the world for the first time. Simply navigating an airport and getting on an airplane for the first time was a major accomplishment. Even though it was a strange new experience, it was also a wonderful time in his life as it gave him a sense of self-worth and confidence. The football experience assured him he could succeed, even if his tasks were untried.

> *I didn't even unpack my bags because I had never played American football. I was certainly big enough and strong enough, I matched up physically, but at the professional level, especially at that most elite level of football in the world, it is not the time you want to*

*start learning the game or even the nuances. So I fig-
ured I wouldn't be there very long. I think that the
inner strength, and just the experiences I learned as a
young boy of never selling myself short, and believing
in myself, and realizing that if I wasn't going to try
what was the point of being there.*

It wasn't long before Andrew drew on his past experiences and started
believing in himself again. He knew that if he wasn't going to try what was
the point in being there. He would just do his best and let the chips fall
where they may, at the very least he knew he could come back to Canada
and play in the CFL. The rest, as they say, is history. Andrew went on to
play with Cincinnati until mid-1987. Andrew's grandfather's teachings
did much to provide stability during these tumultuous football years. He
remembers that if you live well and challenge yourself you will have self-
satisfaction with your life. Life lessons always pick up your spirit and your
courage,

*The step from high school to university is tremendous
in terms of the player's ability, but the step from university to the NFL would be a thousand times greater.
So, you don't know and you learn a lot about yourself
in the journey. I really believe that it is not so much
the destination but the journey. And, if you live well,
and you try to do the things that you have to, to challenge yourself, and to be successful, you learn a lot
about yourself, you learn about your spirit, and you
learn about your courage.*

At age 24, Andrew was went on to play with the *Edmonton
Eskimos*, and played a total of nine seasons for them. "I always thought it
was funny to have an Ojibway playing for the Eskimos!" When asked if
there were any barriers to being a First Nations person in the CFL, Andrew
replied, "ability is the only barrier." Andrew really enjoyed playing in the

CFL. The team was made up of regulars; there was little turnover of new players, everyone was part of the team, and it felt like a real community of athletes. While playing for the *Eskimos*, Andrew became involved with the Players' Association, and began learning about the political workings of the football club, as well as collective agreements, and merchandizing. He soon realized that he didn't know enough about business to make the kind of contributions to the organization that were necessary. So, he went back to school part-time, to learn more about labour economics and how to negotiate proper contracts. He earned his Masters of Business Administration degree (MBA), and through his continued work with the Association, soon gained the knowledge and experience that would assist him in making the transition to another career once his football days were over.

When he left the CFL, Andrew became a volunteer with two high-profile social organizations, Big Brothers/Uncles-at-Large and the Alzheimers Society. He became the national spokesperson for the Alzheimers Society and did nationwide promotion of awareness about this dibilitating disease. It was a personal decision to become involved with the Society; Andrew had two uncles who had suffered from the disease. When the Big Brothers organization came knocking, it was at a time when they were seeking more Aboriginal men to step forward and fill the huge need for role models for Native youth. By his participation, Andrew felt he could give something back to the large Aboriginal community of Edmonton who had been extremely supportive of him throughout his nine years with the *Eskimos*.

> *For me, as my grandfather always taught me, you've got to be comfortable with who you are. You have got to understand the road that your grandmothers and grandfathers have walked before you and there is a strength there, because it allows you to connect with it. Basically you can do whatever you want as long as you are willing to work hard. We all have obstacles placed in our way, whether it is having our language*

152

taken away, or culturally or socially not fitting in. Providing role models is very important to help young people learn some of these values. We must cultivate leadership from our youth. We must make the commitment to our youth because they are one of our greatest resources. It is incumbent on us to encourage, support and provide these opportunity for our young people.

After receiving some notoriety from his association with these two charities, the banks approached Andrew about a career in banking. When he stopped laughing, because he thought he could never fit the corporate banker mold, he realized that it could be a once-in-a-lifetime opportunity. Andrew knew that if you want to learn about banking, you must work in a bank to find out exactly how things are done. Again, he relied on the teachings of his grandfather who used to say, "in order to truly understand and hunt the bear, you must first sleep in its den." Andrew saw that the challenges facing Native people at this time are the lack of understanding of and access to corporate finances, and there is a need to empower Aboriginal people. Andrew knew that it was economic development that would be the key for First Nations people to move forward, while recognizing that the banking institutions simultaneously represented an extension of the hostile government policies that kept Native people in a certain way of life.

Looking at the reserve system and how it was put in place; how the Indian Act restricts a Native person's access to capital for economic development, their ability to build roads or to build a proper home for their children, only served to fuel Andrew's commitment to make things better for First Nations people. Andrew has been successful in supporting land claims, helping the bank understand how to create opportunities for First Nations, and working in partnership with Native people regarding economic development. Andrew has also been active in recruiting Aboriginal people to work in the banks. At last count, eleven Native people have been hired at his bank. He feels that providing someone with the opportunity to have a career, to feed their family, and have a steady income was well worth the efforts. It is ultimately important to Andrew, that Native people have pride, dignity, respect, and an education. One of his primary objectives is to help Native communities understand how banks work, and how to work in partnership with banks,

> *Opportunity means nothing unless we're prepared to realize it. The opportunities are now available because of land claims, because of the ancilliary opportunities that are available as the result of that — if we have the qualified, dynamic, Aboriginal leadership to take control of our own destinies. We talk about self-determination and self-government, but it means nothing unless we are prepared to actually realize these opportunities. I feel that is my role here at the bank. I am trying to help the bank understand how to do business with First Nations, and more importantly, to help the community understand how banks want to do business. It has got to be a partnership — a long-term partnership, moving forward, based on trust. Growing up on Parry Island, or just about any other reserve not that long ago, no one could imagine me or someone like me sitting here as a banker — or a doctor, or a lawyer. It just wasn't an option. But now it is an option and through education we are getting our dignity and respect back. But more importantly we are getting our confidence back as a people. Instead of circumstances dictating what we can or cannot do, we are now saying anything is possible. We are understanding where we have come from, and we are able to target where we want to go, and the journey in between, that's what counts.*

Andrew volunteers his personal time to help improve the community. He is Second Vice-President of the Native Canadian Centre of Toronto and is a member of the Aboriginal Advisory Council at the University of Toronto. He also finds time to assist different Aboriginal groups like Native Child and Family Services where he is helping them set up a craft shop. One of his main ambitions is to be a positive role model and influence on the First Nations community. As a professional athlete he learned very quickly that he had an impact on young people and has used this influence to help youth meet the challenges they face, with an emphasis on seeing their cultural heritage, not as something that impedes their success, but quite to the contrary as an added edge and solid foundation. Andrew is adamant in his belief that we must put a halt to the stereotypical roadblocks that have persisted throughout the years: alcoholism, drug abuse, family violence, suicide, ignorance and illiteracy. In today's society these are neither typical or tolerated by Native people. In the urban setting, Native people are increasingly very dynamic and capable, and developing an extremely strong leadership.

Andrew's family is paramount in his life. He lives in Mississauga, a suburb of Toronto, and has been married ten years. He says, "the Creator has yet to bless us with children, but I'm is still young." His brother and sister live in Toronto and his father, who now lives in Texas, comes home each summer to spend time with his family. His grandmother, Rose, who is 83, lives in Parry Sound. Andrew's grandfather is prominent in his recollections of his youth, and he instilled in Andrew the importance of tradition, culture, spirituality, heritage, and pride in himself, all while grasping the opportunities of the non-Native world, including post-secondary education and a career in the banking business. His teachings have brought Andrew inner peace, strength and the realization that the only barriers to success were the ones we allow to be placed in our path. Andrew's journey is testimony to the courage and determination that are the basis for Aborignal leadership of the future.

Ivy Chaske

"The work I had to do was to be a part of the healing of the people"

Ivy Chaske describes herself as a Dakota woman on all sides, grandmother, grandfather, mother and father. Born in southern Manitoba, her name, "Chaske" (originally "Chaska y") comes from a Dakota way of identifying first males born in a particular family; he would be named *Chaska y.* When you said the name, "people knew that you belonged somewhere," that you had a connection to others before you. Ivy's connection to her Elders and her heritage has been an important part of her life as she has travelled to various places in Canada and the United States, and as she has taken different jobs. A guiding force has been the advice and wisdom of her Elders, especially now as Executive Director of Pedahbun Lodge, an addictions treatment centre in Toronto.

As a younger woman, Ivy spent six years at residential school, but she did not allow her experience to discourage her. She enrolled in the University of Manitoba School of Social Work, studying for a career where she felt she could devote time to her family, and be helpful to Native people. Her path, however, was not exactly as she initially expected,

> *I know what residential school is about, but I think there comes a time when we have to take responsibility. We have to make changes happen in our own lives and in the lives of our people. If I let residential school be a negative in my life then those people who caused me harm will have won in what they tried to do to me -- to destroy the spirit of who I was. I originally started out taking Native Studies and then realized... who would give me a job with a major in Native Studies? I was interested in going into Law, but my three children were very small then. I knew that I needed to spend time with my children, so I decided*

157

*that I needed to choose a career that would allow that.
I decided to focus on social work to get something so
that if I ever needed to raise my children on my own I
could do that. I had a very supportive husband and I
was working as well. I'd go to work at midnight, get
home at 8:00, get my kids off to school, say hello and
goodbye to my husband, and go to university. When it
was slow at work, I'd do my reading on the job.*

Ivy found the most difficult thing about university was not the studying
or work, but the incredible racism in the curriculum and at the school. A lot
of the information the university presented about Aboriginal people was
very stereotypical, citing them as people full of problems. Disillusioned, she
left university for awhile (but not before telling them off). Eventually she
went back again, and the Dean told her that they would do anything they
could to help her. But she knew that changing the thinking of the university
and the professors was his job, not hers. That made it easier for her to finish.
She concentrated on getting her degree, and decided it wasn't up to her to
fight them; that she had more important work to do with her own people.

Ivy's experience at the university was an eye-opener for her, and a big
disappointment. She thought she would meet people there who would
challenge her to really learn, to think, and be critical and analytical, to move
beyond herself. But, she ended up feeling she was smarter than some of the
people who were teaching her, and that if she was going to learn anything
in this world, she was going to have to teach herself, to take responsibility
for herself and what she needed to know.

When Ivy graduated and started working in social work, she held many
different positions in Native communities, making many trips back and forth
between Toronto and Manitoba. In the early 1980s, she was in Toronto
doing employment counselling and was very involved in the Native
community. One of her jobs involved running a coffee house,

*In the first five years I was here I ran a coffee house
because I felt there was a need for a place where*

Native people could get together and have no connection with alcohol or drugs. Just a place to be together; where people could care about each other. I ran it with no government money whatsoever. It was totally community supported, with volunteers. If we didn't have the money for the rent, we would have a cover charge, but if you didn't have any money, you could come and work for a bit and stay the rest of the night. Nobody was ever turned away. We had people come through and perform too. There were a lot of people who were doing well in the arts, and they would do pieces of their plays, poetry, music, all kinds of things. It was an incredible, amazing, creative time.

At the same time Ivy became a member of the Board of Directors of the Native Canadian Centre, and also founded the Native Woman's Resource Centre. Ivy explains how this came about,

One night we decided to have just Aboriginal women performers at the coffee house. It was so successful that we decided to have a festival. We did a four-day festival called Aboriginal Women in the Arts which showcased Aboriginal women from across the country. It was incredible! When the festival ended we were on such a high from the strength and the knowledge, and the things that we could give each other as Native women, that I said we need a place where we can always be together to do that, to be there for each other. And it was from that, that the Native Women's Resource Centre was born.

Keeping the Resource Centre going was not easy, as funding would come and go. For a while, Ivy kept it going with her contract work salary while she lived with friends to save rent. During this time Ivy was also very much involved in the mainstream women's movement. She worked very hard to have Native women's voices represented in the movement, but found it to be a frustrating and disillusioning experience. As she explained,

> *I was very much involved in the women's movement and I made a conscious decision not to be involved anymore. I really felt that I couldn't be a part of a movement that excluded my brothers, my uncles, my grandfathers, my nephews. I strongly felt their exclusion, as well as the racism within the women's movement. I came to the realization that I was a token Indian. When I spoke and they agreed with me, they expected that I spoke on behalf of all Native women; but when I said something that was different than what they wanted to hear, then they suddenly questioned my representation of Native women's perspectives. I told them I sit on five Boards of Aboriginal community organizations who have mandated me to speak on behalf of the women in the community. I became very disillusioned with all the rhetoric, the tokenism, the racism and that I was forever taking care of their women's guilt, and I had more important things to do. I realized that I'm here on this earth for a very short time and my life, everyone's life, is sacred. I needed to take that life and spend that time with my people.*

Ivy returned to Winnipeg and for five years was very active in the Aboriginal community there. She helped set up the first housing co-op for Aboriginal women and their children. She helped in the formation of a women's shelter and a transition shelter. She started teaching journalism in colleges and universities in Winnipeg, and she became involved with the Hollow-Water Project which gained national recognition for healing circles and help with sexual abuse. She was with Hollow-Water for two years as a trainer and community worker. One achievement that Ivy is very proud of in Winnipeg was her involvement with a radio show. Once again, she was involved with the arts,

> *I sat on a Board called Native Media Network. It was mostly men on that Board, only two women. Every time I put a motion forward they'd defeat it! But part of their mandate, and they were funded by the government to do this, was to put women's programs on the radio show that they had. Of course they didn't include women's programming. The other woman on the Board and I were always fighting with the guys about it. Finally the President said to me, if you don't like it then do your own radio show. So I did. I had no idea how to run a radio show, no idea whatsoever, but I remembered meeting this woman from the CBC, a broadcaster, and I gave her a call. I asked her if she would volunteer her time to teach us how to produce a radio show, and she said, "sure." With the help of equipment borrowed from the community college on the weekend, she taught us how to do production work, all the technical stuff, the editing, everything. It was amazing.*

None of the women involved had ever done anything like this before. Ivy and her group found the money (air time then was about $200 per hour) and bought the air time. The men's show was on before them, but because Ivy had found non-governmental funding to support her show, when government funds were cut, her show continued when others were cut, "Not only did we stay on the air but I won a Human Rights Journalism award from Manitoba for the radio program; I did a show on homosexuality in the Aboriginal community, and it was really an interesting show."

At the same time, Ivy helped found an organization called the Aboriginal Women's Network which was geared not to be a service organization but an actual resource for Aboriginal women, "We started an archive; we did training and professional development; we did mentoring and really positive stuff, empowering things, different kinds of programs." Ivy also got an opportunity to go to Africa for the International Decade for Women. Four Aboriginal women went, and they made a video about it. They had first hired some people to make it for them, but they were not happy with the results so they decided to teach themselves how to do it. With the help of a video pool for artists in Winnipeg, they taught themselves and other interested Aboriginal artists how to work with video. Ivy says,

> *I wanted to learn video, learn how to do a radio show, and I wanted to broadcast. I wanted to learn all those things, but it's very difficult for me to do something just for me. I wasn't raised that way. I came from a family of hereditary leaders. From the time you are very young, you're taught to think for the people. So I couldn't just do it for me, I had to teach others and bring them along. With a lot of things that I do, I drag people along to learn so that they are aware and knowledgeable and it is less scary to do things.*

Ivy came back to Toronto and once again became a leader in the Aboriginal community. Her years in Winnipeg, all her experiences with community organizations, her traditional background, and with expressing herself through the arts taught her the value of recognizing her own gifts and how to give them back. Before she took the position of Executive Director at Pedahbun Lodge she went to see her Elders to help guide her and let her know if this was the right decision,

> *Whenever I get asked to do anything I talk to a group of old women who give me direction from that point. They're not afraid to tell you if they think that you're letting your ego grab hold of you, or if you're letting power get hold of you, or if you're letting other things*

*get in the way of the work you're supposed to do.
Recently, one of the Elders advised me that something
I wanted to do wasn't a good thing, that our teaching
s are not to be made public in that way. I had been
asked to speak about them. She said, you know it's
your responsibility; you can do it if you want to. When
I said, maybe I'll do it, she said, "but remember, I still
have my red willow stick." So I thought, "on second
thought, I won't do it!"*

Ivy's work, and the things she does in the community are very much determined by the Elders. She says she doesn't speak to the Elders because it is the "in" thing, but because she was brought up with them, "I understand that they are there to give me direction, that they have the wisdom to show me clearly when my vision is not clear, and to hear when I'm not hearing clearly, and to speak in a good way, because that's not always easy, especially when you're in the city."

Ivy now lives in Toronto with her grandmother and her daughter. Her daughter is a field supervisor for a child welfare agency. Her other daughter lives with her dad. Her son is going to the University of Manitoba, and recently got a job to promote a Youth Project. Ivy speaks her language fluently, and married her husband, a Dene man, in part because he was fluent in his language and came from a strong family. She emphasizes the value language and traditions, and explained that the combined marriage resulted in her children having a little of both languages and traditions, but because her husband and she had to communicate in English, perhaps the children didn't have the opportunity to learn as much as they could if they had been consistently raised in one of their parents' cultures. Ivy cited her own experience and from her observations how critical these factors are, "Let's get back on track with these things, because you can lose it in one generation, with English; that's where I talk about having responsibility -- if there is not instruction in your Native language, see if you can find it for your children." Ivy's children have carried on her interest in helping the community, but Ivy sees carrying on that helping in the community as well as maintaining one's Native languages as an issue of personal responsibility. Referring to a friend who had his children taken away by the Children's Aid Society and who did not have the chance to learn their language, Ivy said,

> *Even though these things have happened, he still has that responsibility. That kind of responsibility, for me, is something that I feel really strong about. Maybe it's just my age. I am tired of whining and complaining. I think we need to tell the truth. Because if we don't, that stuff will happen again, and in order to speak the truth we have to say what really happened. And try and change it.*

Ivy wants to go home and be with her Elders eventually, but she says she'll know when its time. As yet, there is a tremendous amount of work to be done. As she gets older, she remembers the power of the land and the reason that the Elders stay home and on the land. It increases their contact with the spirit world that they came from. It is where they get their strength. When she's ready, she'll go back and help them too, because as she says, "if it wasn't for them I wouldn't be doing the things I do. I wouldn't be strong enough."

In the meantime, Ivy is helping the Toronto Aboriginal community, women, men and children, and maybe just a little bit, the Aboriginal Spirit of the world. She continues to learn, to value her culture and her Elders, and offers that as a model for others, not with ego, but with reality. She encourages Aboriginal people to remember their culture, to go after that learning, and to not be afraid. It is there to be done!

Notes on the Contributors

A. Rodney Bobiwash is Anishnawbe from the Mississauga First Nation. He has lived in Toronto for ten years where he has actively been involved in urban self-government iniatives, and anti-racism work particularly in relation to anti-Indian organizing. He graduated from Trent University and studied at the University of Oxford, England, specializing in fur-trade era history. For the last three years, he has been the Director of First Nations House at the University of Toronto, and teaches there in the Aboriginal Studies Program.

Barbara A. Gajic is Anishnawbekwe of the Nipissing First Nation. She is 54 years old and in the third year of her Bachelor's Degree at the University of Toronto. She is majoring in Aboriginal Studies, with a Minor in History. Her future plans include writing, and continuing her studies of Aboriginal history and culture in Canada.

Eleanor Hill is originally from the Six Nations of the Grand River Territory. She graduated from Jarvis Collegiate and worked for many years with the Toronto advertising firm Young & Rubicam Ltd. Upon her retirement she returned to Six Nations with her husband and daughter where she is currently an active grandmother of two. Besides volunteering at the Iroquois Nursing Home, she is a member of the Ojistoh Seniors Club as well as serving on the committee for the C. Ruby Smith-Sears Memorial Educational Scholarship Fund. Her accomplished efforts in sewing, knitting, and canning have made her a keen competitor in the Agricultural Society also known as the Six Nations Fair. Eleanor also finds time to enjoy golfing and performing with the Mohawk Singers.

Heather Howard-Bobiwash, originally from the Eastern Townships of Quebec, has lived in Toronto for three years where she has worked as the Editor of the Native Canadian Newsletter of the Native Canadian Centre of Toronto. She is very active in the Native community in a number of projects, including the Toronto Native Community History Project. She has completed a Masters Degree in Social/Cultural Anthropology from the University of Toronto, and is currently pursuing her PhD. Her research focuses on women's invovlement in Native community development and cultural identity continuity in urban contexts. She is also co-editing a volume on feminist anthropology which will be published by Broadview Press.

Contributors

Lorraine Le Camp is of James Bay Cree ancestry (Moose Factory). She operated her own graphic design and illustration studio, and raised a daughter and a son before returning to academia where she obtained her B.A. and B.Ed. from York University. She then completed a Masters degree and is currently working on her Doctorate in Sociology at the Ontario Institute for Studies in Education at the University of Toronto. Besides presenting lectures, holding seminars, organizing group activities and volunteering with local community groups, Lorraine also teaches a course at Seneca College.

Roger Obonsawin is a member of the Abenaki Nations whose First Nation base is in Quebec and Northeastern United States. He is an outspoken advocate of Aboriginal rights, particularly for urban people. He is the President of the O.I. Group of Companies providing consulting and personnel development services to First Nations organizations across Canada. He has served as Executive Director of the Native Canadian Centre of Toronto, and the Red Lake Indian Friendship Centre, as well as founding President of the National Association of Friendship Centres, and Pedahbun Lodge, a substance abuse treatment centre in Toronto.

Frances Sanderson is Anishnawbekwe of the Whitefish First Nation (Birch Island). She is the Executive Director of Nishnawbe Homes Inc., an Aboriginal non-profit housing organization in Toronto. A very active volunteer in both non-Native and Native communities, she is also a member of the Board of Directors of the Native Canadian Centre of Toronto, and of the boards of several other Native organizations in Toronto.

Suzanne Stiegelbauer
Suzanne M. Stiegelbauer is an Associate Professor at the Ontario Institute for Studies in Education of the University of Toronto. She is a past member of the Board of Directors of the Native Canadian Centre of Toronto (1987-1993), and is currently on the board of Aboriginal Legal Services of Toronto.. Her PhD thesis with the University of Texas at Austin, entitled, "The Road Back to the Future: Tradition and the Involvement of Elders at the Native Canadian Centre of Toronto" resulted from community-based research she conducted in conjunction with the development of the NCCT Elders and Traditional Teachers' Council. She is co-author of two books on educational change and reform in schools.

Index

A

Aboriginal inherent rights 29
Aboriginal Legal Services of Toronto
    91, 101
Aboriginal Women's Network 159
Aboriginal Peacekeeping Unit 110, 117
addictions -- alcohol and drugs, *and*
    alternatives 159, *and* Birds of a
    Feather (AA) 143, *and* counsel-
    ling 34, *and* homeless, *and*
    incarceration 102, 124, *and*
    residential school 126, 129, *and*
    treatment 157, 162
agriculture 7
Ahbenoojeyug the Native Children's
    Program 37, 40
Algonquian 8, 11
Algonquin 8, Golden Lake 107
American Indian Movement 37
American Revolutionary War 14
Anduhyaun Inc. 121
Anishnawbe 1-4, 8, 10, 86
Anishnawbe Health Centre 123, 124
Archaeologists 7, 8, 10
Arriaga, Winona 65
assimilation 19

B

B.C. Indian Position Paper, "Brown
    Paper" 38
Bagot Commission 18
Ball, Margaret 61
banking 153
Battle of Moraviantown 18
Bay of Quinte 14
Bear Robe, Andrew 37
Beaulieu, Fran 49
Benai, Eddie Benton 7, 22, 71
Benedict, Ernie 76

Bill C-31 29, 47, 48
Blackbird, Bill 61
Blackfoot 9
Brant, Clare 40
British 13, 14 (*See also* English)
Brule, Etienne 10
burial grounds 17
Butler, Col. John 15, 17

C

Canadian Association in Solidarity
    with Native Peoples, *See* Indian
    Eskimo Association
Canadian Constitution (Section 91) 92
Canadian Constitution Act 56
Canadian Dept. of Citizenship 31
Canadian Indian Centre of Toronto
    62, *(See also* Native Canadian
    Centre of Toronto)
Canadian National Exhibition 11
Cape Croker 33
Capton, Delma 31, 62
Carter, D. Le M. 31
Champlain, Samuel de 5
Chretien, Jean 38
Christian, Dorothy 72
Christian Island 26
Christianity 11, 19, *and* the Church
    102, 127
citizenship 92
Civilized Tribes of the Chippewa 19
Clark, William 15
Coat of Arms, City of Toronto 17
Collins, John 15
colony 12, 17, *and* Native participation
    in 20
Commanda, Mary 61
commerce 7
community service 133-34, 142, 152,
    163

"commuter" lifestyle 85
consciousness-raising 37-41 38, 51
Coppoway, George 19
Corbiere-Lavell, Jeanette 48
Council Grounds, Mississauga 18
Covenant Chain 10, 12
Credit River 15, 17
Cree 8
culture 7 (*See also* Native Canadian
    Centre of Toronto *and* cultural
    programming, *and* Traditional
    Awareness Gathering), *and*
    homeless 129, *and* identity 25,
    28, 29 (*See also* identity), *and*
    inmates and ex-offenders 110,
    and philosophy about hunting
    116, *and* traditional teaching 118,
    123, 124, 133, 137, 142, 149, *and*
    youth 153

D

Dakota 157
Dene Chipewyan 115
Detroit 14, 18
Dick, Jimmy 51, 57
Dorchester, Lord 15
Drew, Douglas 61
Dumont, Jim 70, 72
Dutch 9, 10, 11

E

Eagle Feather 113
Eagleheart Drum 51, 52
Eaton, Mrs. John David 31, 35
economic development 153-154
education 65-85
Elders 75, 103, 137-138, 144, 157, 162-
    164 (*See also* Native Canadian
    Centre of Toronto *and* Elders and
    Traditional Teachers' Council)

employment, *and* steelwork 98-99, *and*
    construction 100, *and* choices
    116
Enemikeese 6, 22
English 9
epidemics 11
ethnostress 85
Etobicoke 15, 21
European Economic Community 92
ex-offenders 112
explorers 1, 5, 10

F

Family Needs Study 45
family and parenting 119-121, 142, 146-
    147
Federated Brotherhood
First Nations House, University of
    Toronto 144
foster care (Children's Aid Society),
    102, 107, 113, 127
French 9, 11, 13
Friendship Centre Movement 30, *and*
    friendship centres 135
Friendship Club 62
fur trade 5, 10, 11, 21

G

Gabriel Dumont non-profit housing 85
governance 89
Gradual Civilization Act of 1857 19
Grand River 14
Great Lakes 9, 10, 21, 22 (*See also*
    Mishomis Book)
Great Migration 8
Greenberg, Lila 61

H

habitat 5
Hager, Alvin 28, 58

spirituality 11
sports 149-150, *and* Canadian Football
    League 149, 151, 152
St. George Society 112-113
Steinhauer, Henry Bird 19
stereotypes 44, 85, 127
Stinson, Art 61
Stoney Point First Nation 123, 125
storytelling 66
Street Patrol 123-129, *and* volunteers
    127
subsistence 6
Sunday, John 19
Sylvester, Hettie
    26, 27, 44, 58, 59, 64

T

Taddle Creek 15
Techumseth 18
Teiaiagon 10
Toronto Indian Club
    26, 27, 29, 30, 60-64
Toronto Islands 5
Toronto Native Times 35, 41
trade 5-9, 13-14, *and* networks (Abo-
    riginal) 11
treaties 11, Gunshot Treaty 21, Peace
    and Friendship Treaties 14,
    Williams Treaties 15, 91
Trudeau, Pierre E. 38
Turner, James 31
Turner, Pat 33, 61
Two Row Wampum 9
Two-Axe Early, Mary 48
Tyendinaga Mohawk Territory 86

U

Umprevill, Danny 61
Union of Ontario Indians 36, 37
United Way 35

University of Toronto 17
University Women's Club 39
Upper Canada 18
"Urban Indians" 38, 97
Urban Society (Vancouver) 90

V

VanEvery, Dolores 61
Vet, Danny 60
veterans, World Wars, 2, 3, 27

W

Walpole Island 20, 61
War of 1812 14
Wausausking First Nation 149
Western Sanitorium 62
Wheatley, Fred 35, 55, 59, 61, 76
White Paper on Indian Policy 38, 87
Whitefish First Nation (Birch Island)
    27, 131
Wigwamen Housing Corp. 37, 41
Wikwemikong 48
Wilson, Margaret 60
women 27, 29, 47, 159 (*See also* Native
    Canadian Centre of Toronto *and*
    Ladies Auxiliary), *and* Women's
    Movement 161-162

Y

Y.M.C.A. 26, 29, 61
York, town of 18, 19
youth 3, 35, 48, 66-69, 74, 142, 143,
    144-145

172